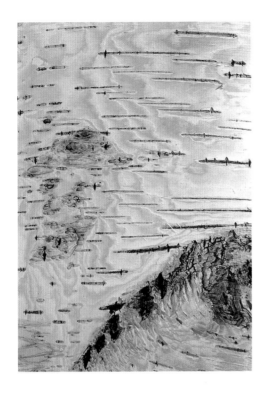

Wild NEW YORK

A Celebration of Our State's Natural Beauty

Text by Charles Brumley
Photography by Carl E. Heilman II
Foreword by Bill McKibben

Voyageur Press

First published in 2005 by Voyageur Press, an imprint of MBI Publishing Company, Galtier Plaza, Suite 200, 380 Jackson Street, St. Paul, MN 55101-3885 USA

Edited by Josh Leventhal
Designed by Andrea Rud
Printed in China

05   06   07   08   09   5   4   3   2   1

Library of Congress Cataloging-in-Publication Data

Brumley, Charles.
  Wild New York : a celebration of our state's natural beauty / text by Charles Brumley ; photography by Carl E. Heilman II ; foreword by Bill McKibben.
      p. cm.
  Includes bibliographical references and index.
  ISBN-13 978-0-89658-663-5
  ISBN-10 0-89658-663-4 (hardcover)
  1. New York (State)--Pictorial works. 2. New York (State)--History, Local--Pictorial works. 3. Natural history--New York (State) 4. Natural history--New York (State)--Pictorial works. 5. Natural areas--New York (State)--Pictorial works. 6. New York (State)--Description and travel. I. Heilman, Carl, 1954- II. Title.
  F120.B78 2005
  917.47'02--dc22
                     2005011708

MBI titles are also available at discounts in bulk quantity for industrial or sales-promotional use. For details write to Special Sales Manager at MBI Publishing Company, Galtier Plaza, Suite 200, 380 Jackson Street, St. Paul, MN 55101-3885 USA.

On the front cover: Fall colors are at their peak along the Niagara River gorge at Whirlpool State Park near Buffalo.

On page 1: The waters of Enfield Creek settle into a quiet pool after cascading down Lucifer Falls in Robert H. Treman State Park, near Ithaca.

On page 2: The heaving waves of Lake Ontario form frozen sculptures in winter on the shoreline in front of the eroded "badlands" at Chimney Bluffs State Park.

On page 3: Mountain laurel bloom in Storm King State Park, overlooking the Hudson River toward Storm King Mountain and Breakneck Ridge.

On page 4: The so-called Walking Dunes at Hither Hills State Park are a distinctive feature of Long Island's eastern tip.

On page 5: Layers of fog form over the valleys and among the mountains of the Adirondacks' western High Peaks, as viewed from the top of St. Regis Mountain.

On page 6: This idyllic forest stream flows within one of the world's largest cities: Richmond Stream is located in Egbertville Ravine in New York City's Staten Island Greenbelt.

On page 7, clockwise from upper left: The beauty of the Adirondacks can be seen in the details: the distinctive bark of a white birch, near the Adirondack Loj at Heart Lake; water droplets clinging to the needles of a white pine after a summer rain in Brant Lake; grasses and a weathered pine tree near Streeter Pond; mushrooms growing among the fallen autumn leaves on the trail to Pharaoh Mountain.

On page 8: Catskill Park is a nature lover's paradise throughout the year. These multi-seasonal views from Sunset Rock look south to North-South Lake and the eastern escarpment of the Catskill Mountains.

On page 9: The wild ocean surf at Jones Beach is less than an hour from midtown Manhattan.

On page 10: Passing storm clouds glow in the last light of day over the Fulton Chain of Lakes in the central Adirondacks, looking west from the Bald Mountain fire tower.

On page 11, inset: A red eft scurries across the moss at the edge of an Adirondack stream.

Acknowledgments

I WISH TO thank first and foremost my wife, Karen Loffler, for her unerring in-house editorial skill, and for impressing on me that this assignment would be not only fun but perhaps even a little important.

Josh Leventhal, my editor at Voyageur Press, took over where Karen left off and provided much guidance and many valuable midcourse corrections.

And last but certainly not least, I would like to thank Carl Heilman, both a wonderfully talented photographer and a good friend who has done me so many favors. I have known Carl for about twenty years and have long been aware of his photographic skills from his Adirondack work. His talented artist's eye was most impressed upon me when we began to explore how to approach this book, and the results are obvious as you enjoy the following pages.

— Charles Brumley

FIRST, THANKS MUCH to my wife, Meg, and my daughter, Greta, for the times they held up the fort, for companionship sometimes, and for reading the map on my many excursions across the state—and for all the behind-the-scenes work that allowed me to photograph for the book.

Many thanks to Josh Leventhal at Voyageur Press for offering the project to me, and for his pleasant, efficient, and patient demeanor in setting up the project—and keeping it on track.

Thanks especially to my friend of many years, Chuck Brumley, whose thoughtful authoring sets the mood and gives a much fuller meaning to the diverse images of the wonderful landscape that is New York State. And also my gratitude to author and friend, Bill McKibben, whose eloquence with words provides such a wonderful sense of place while presenting the challenges these wild places face.

I would like to thank the staff of the New York State offices of The Nature Conservancy, especially Connie Prickett, who set up contacts for me throughout the state. Regional staff members who were quite helpful include Jim Howe, Kirstin Seelen, Marie Palagonia, Lucy Cutler, Sharon Pickett, Ann Gambling, Laura Vandermark Lynch, Rod Christie, Mike Laspin, and Mike Scheibel.

Thank you also to Ken Rimany, Willie Janeway, Bob DeVilleneuve of *The Conservationist*, Patti Coan, Barbara Drake, Julie Ball and staff of the Adirondack Council, the Adirondack Mountain Club, the Association for the Protection of the Adirondacks, Audubon, the Natural History Museum of the Adirondacks, and many others with whom I have been in contact through this project. A special thank you to John Sagendorf, Jeff DeGroff, and the folks at Howe Caverns, and Cindy Smith at Rock City Park for their kind help and permission to photograph these special places.

And last but certainly not least, many thanks to all the folks who helped with suggestions of locations or contacts. There are many whose names I never learned that I met in traveling and who offered thoughts that led me to unusual and unique locations.

— Carl E. Heilman

CONTENTS

FOREWORD

by Bill McKibben

Bill McKibben has lived most of his life in the Adirondacks. His most recent book is *Wandering Home: A Long Walk Through America's Most Hopeful Landscape, Vermont's Champlain Valley and New York's Adirondacks.*

I HAVE NOT the slightest doubt that New York is the best kept natural secret among the fifty states. It has absolutely everything. I know and love the Adirondacks best: they are a western-scale wilderness in the east. But the lower Hudson Valley was so lovely it launched an entire artistic movement. The Finger Lakes, cradled in the undulating landscape of central New York, are the equals of any lakes on earth for sheer quiet beauty. Long Island with its ring of sandy barrier shores is as lovely as the capes of Massachusetts or the Carolinas. Lake Erie and Lake Ontario are inland seas. Niagara Falls was the first place that Americans located the sublime, long before they found the geysers of Yellowstone or the granite cliffs of Muir's Yosemite.

And those are just the places that everyone already knows about. There's so much more: the Tug Hill Plateau, snowiest corner of the east, where the fat flakes hurry out of the sky to make room for more; or the Thousand Islands, or the sloping hill farms on the edge of Lake Champlain, or the thousand streams pouring out of the Catskills down cataract and chute, headed toward the mighty Hudson. Or even the fringes of New York City, those strands of beach that in the right seasons are awash with horseshoe crabs intent on mating. Or even the very centers of the great city—Central Park, Prospect Park, Van Cortlandt Park—where the migrating birds drop with such relief as they catch sight of green islands in the stretching gray.

It's not just that New York *has* wild places. It's that New Yorkers have done so much to preserve, restore, and enhance them. The Adirondacks, for instance, is the single largest experiment in biological restoration on the face of the earth, six million acres returned to health by the century-long forbearance and wisdom of the people of the Empire State. There are few signs that this bipartisan determination is flagging; this past year alone saw tens of thousands of acres added to the state's "Forever Wild" holdings, and tens of thousands more set aside under easement to remain as working forests. Such big projects are echoed in the work of land trusts and nature conservancies in every county of the state. The gorgeous photos contained within these pages bear witness to human foresight just as surely as they bear witness to the wonders of evolution and to the play of water and time on rock.

This splendid state deserves a book as lovely as this, and it deserves as well the devoted attention of its citizens. Relax with this volume of an evening; in the morning lace up your boots and head out.

Above
Morning light cuts through the fog on an early summer day near the outlet of St. Regis Pond in the Adirondacks.

Facing page
The waters of Verkeerder Kill Falls gently trickle over the edge of the eastern escarpment on Sam's Point Dwarf Pine Preserve in the Shawangunk Mountains of southern New York.

INTRODUCTION

Above
In late May and early June, pink lady's slippers are a common sight in certain habitats in the forest and along open ridges in the Adirondacks.

Left
An exposed rock ledge on the eastern summit of Black Dome provides a view south over the Catskill Forest Preserve.

The Deer River flows through the Littlejohn State Wildlife Management Area on the Tug Hill Plateau, one of the state's most underappreciated wilderness areas.

ABOUT FORTY MILES southwest from my home in Saranac Lake in the Adirondacks of New York is the northern boundary of Hamilton County. Deep in the heart of the Adirondack Park, Hamilton County, spread over 1,745 square miles, is home to just over five thousand people—and no stop lights. Not one.

Go south another 250 miles from my home and you're in New York City, with millions of people and countless stoplights. These downstate New Yorkers are all an easy day's drive from my home. Add yet more miles to reach, say, Philadelphia, Baltimore, and Washington, D.C., and you've included ever more millions within a day's drive of the six-million-acre state park where I live.

And there's the rub—those millions. Where, in this teeming, writhing modern world shall such multitudes go to recreate? To *re-create*? To seek solitude, peace, and restorative quiet? If they come to New York, they need not seek just Hamilton County, nor even the Adirondacks. Within each of the state's sixty-two counties can be found a spot for respite and solitude—and a chance for re-creation. Somewhere close by—maybe hidden, perhaps jealously guarded as a cherished secret but in fact open to all—is a park, or preserve, or refuge.

These wild parks are scattered across New York's six-hundred-mile breadth, a span from Montauk Point on far eastern Long Island to the Pennsylvania line at Lake Erie. The variety in topography, geology, flora and fauna, and human history in this realm almost beggars description.

How shall we know of the cherished places? In almost as many ways as there are places: by our own travel, in history books and guidebooks—and here, in a book of magnificent photographs that evince wonder, a desire to see these places for ourselves, or even nostalgia for a place we've never been.

But the challenges to knowing New York's beauty and its origins are daunting. For example, how far back in time do you want to go? Just understanding the geology of the state could be a lifetime pursuit. Many of geology's terms are not even in our everyday lexicon. You have to pick your cocktail party to throw around rock-related terms such as *igneous* and *anorthosite*, eras such as Cambrian and Pleistocene, and glacier-related terms such as *drumlins* and *moraines*. On a frequent if not everyday basis in the Adirondacks, you might hear or use the terms *erratics* (boulders seemingly in the middle of nowhere, dropped by a retreating glacier far from any massive parent rock) and *eskers* (sandy ridges that were once underground glacial streams).

If you live in the Big Apple, you might learn that some of the success of New York City is due not just to the city's fortuitous location at the nexus of major waterways, but its underpinnings as well: Fordham gneiss, Inwood limestone, and Manhattan schist are all tough and relatively resistant to erosion and form a strong rock foundation for skyscrapers.

Geology plays a role in other ways, too. In modern times, a variety of geological sources have brought economic gain to the state, including paint pigment

from red iron ore, as well as salt, gypsum, limestone for cement, sand and gravel for concrete, and clay for brick.

A partial rainbow highlights the eastern sky between passing storm clouds and the foaming waves along the Fire Island National Seashore.

And that's just down in the ground. When we come up a little higher, of course, we see trees. The state has about 150 species of trees, most of which are indigenous. From New York's mountains to her sea, the trees seem to come from two different worlds. On Long Island, the names of the trees sound as though they might have been taken from the southern saga *Gone With the Wind*: laurel magnolia, sweet gum, and hop trees. Moving west we find nut-bearing trees such as oaks, hickories, and chestnut. (The chestnuts are second-growth trees or rare survivors of the blight that came by way of Long Island at the turn of the twentieth century.) At higher elevations, maples, birches, beeches, spruces, white pines, and hemlocks predominate. Above the Adirondack tree line are less than one hundred acres of fragile and rare alpine flora. Here grow delicate bearberry willow and Lapland rose bay.

From a human viewpoint, you can almost imagine the contrast evolving through the ages, from Native American travelers thinking, "What a great canoe (or basket) *that* birch would make," to modern New York City–ites paying dearly for a decorative stack of pristine white birch logs to sit unburned in an apartment fireplace. (Or one Adirondacker's misguided and failed attempt to transplant a magnolia to Saranac Lake, as I did.)

The first light of the day bathes the eastern Adirondack High Peaks with a warm glow. Mount Haystack and the steep, rocky walls of Panther Gorge are prominent in the foreground of this view from Mount Marcy, the state's highest peak.

You might also want to pick your season as you seek the "true" New York. Just as true today as when written in 1940 for the book *New York: A Guide to the Empire State* is this description of the state's spring and summer glory:

In forest areas many species of flowering plants pop up where light and rainfall permit. Wild sarsaparilla, Solomon's seal, bunchberry, star flower, trillium, enchanter's nightshade, sweet-scented bedstraw, Indian pipe, and goldthread are not uncommon. Over the greater part of the state, meadow flowers often form pied blankets acres in extent. Dandelions, cut as weeds from lawns, grow a foot tall on road shoulders, framing black macadam in borders of gold. Queen Anne's lace, devil's paint brush, white daisy, and black-eyed Susan bloom concurrently in bottom valleys, forming a tapestry of green, white, yellow, and orange. Buttercups are blended in grassy openings with violets, strawberry blooms, and clover. Goldenrod and wild rose (the state flower) hug the borders of woodlots. Cattails and blue flag thrive in tidal flats of the Hudson estuary; rushes, cut for chair bottoms, cover acres of the Finger Lakes shallows; and alders grow at the water's edge between the white and yellow water lilies and the dry shores of Adirondack lakes.

While our geological foundations have existed for many eons, and our flora and fauna for many thousands of years before the arrival of man, once man did come, changes on the land came fast. After the American Revolution, settlement extended northward and westward from New York City and the Hudson River Valley. New Englanders, French Canadians, and French émigrés settled the North Country. Others traveled the Mohawk and Cherry Valley routes to the state's interior.

The years on either side of 1800 were New York's frontier period. Soon after the War of 1812, the commercial interests from the central and western parts of the state, trying to stay competitive, used the natural waterways to get their products to lucrative markets: down the Delaware to Philadelphia, down the Susquehanna to Baltimore, and down the St. Lawrence to Montreal.

De Witt Clinton saw that a canal connecting the Hudson River with the Great Lakes would fold the western farmers into competitive eastern markets. Goods sent down the Hudson to New York City would give the city commercial pre-eminence. After the Erie Canal opened in 1825, the cost of hauling a ton of freight from Buffalo to New York City dropped from $120 to $14.

The economic climate, however, was perhaps overly heady with desire for development. Near the end of the nineteenth century, for example, Niagara Falls was well on its way to almost total commercialization. Ugly buildings were all over the margin.

In 1885, during the presidency of Grover Cleveland, Congress passed a bill that protected the Falls. The purchase of property by a state for purely aesthetic purposes was a new development in land use, with significance not only for the falls but for park policy throughout the country. Places so cherished today began to get their first, tentative protections following Niagara Falls' lead.

The rapid increases in urbanization and commercialization that created problems during the latter part of the nineteenth century continue to be a challenge today, as the desire to set aside land for environmental protection generates its own set of political problems. The numbers give away the challenges: In her slightly over 47,000 square miles, New York has roughly four

A frog peers up from the mat of a floating sphagnum bog on Moxham Pond in the central Adirondacks.

A Hornbeck canoe is beached on a sandbar in front of mergansers swimming along the marsh grasses of the Ausable Marsh State Wildlife Management Area on Lake Champlain.

hundred people in each square mile; the United States overall has only eighty. Kings and Queens counties, each with well over two million people, are practically bulging at the seams.

True, the highest population areas are clustered in and near New York City. But the pressures of highly urbanized living make one yearn for an outlet. During the years I worked as an Adirondack guide—hiking, canoeing, camping, and fishing—I came to know a number, 212, that to me represented the need for that outlet. For 212 is the area code for Manhattan. A phone message with that area code on my answering machine, asking for information about my services, often meant I was about to have a quietly desperate Manhattanite on my hands, ready for a change of pace and scenery. When they came, they wanted me to show them the nooks and crannies that only a local could know, the quiet places away from the teeming hordes, the places not found in the guidebooks.

The book you hold in your hands puts me in mind of such places. It isn't a guidebook—at least in the usual sense—containing directions for how to get to specific places and what to look for when you get there. The places shown here are not secrets. They are accessible, most of them are free, and they are, well, yours in every sense of the word.

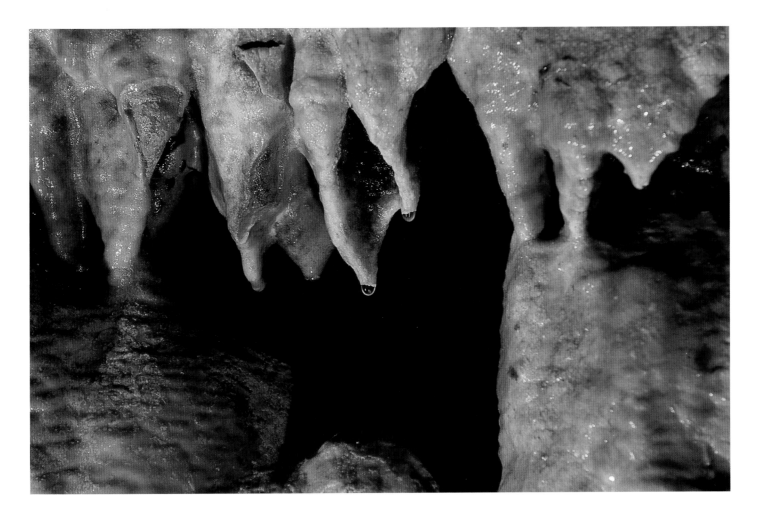

But perhaps this *is* a guidebook in a wider, visceral, more introspective sense. Carl Heilman's evocative photographs capture the moods, the colors, the sense of wind, and sun, and water, of places across New York from Montauk to Lake Erie.

When Carl and I first discussed this book, we asked each other, how should we jointly conceptualize it? I was thinking of a hopefully ordered jumble of history, ecology, and geology, filtered through my own experiences throughout the state; Carl was envisioning landscapes—light, colors, moods, and expanses. He seized, perhaps subconsciously, on geology as a fundamental basis for landscapes. The vision was somewhere in the middle—but likely evoked the best from each of us.

You will have your own emotions and reactions as you look and read and feel, as you should. You may even be moved to some sort of action, such as joining a group that protects these areas or working in your own way to preserve the beauty of the land.

You may begin to understand your connections with the unspoiled parks, preserves, and refuges that exist for us to enjoy throughout New York.

As you ask yourself how shall we know such places, you may answer, "Ponder, wonder—and go."

Howe Caverns near Albany is one of the state's most popular natural attractions, with hundreds of stalactites and stalagmites within the winding underground passageways.

"There is one river which, from its source to the ocean, unrolls along chain of landscapes wherein there is no tame feature, but each successive view presents new combinations of beauty and majesty . . . and its name is, the Hudson."
—Bayard Taylor, 1860

Chapter 1

From the Wilderness to the Sea

The Hudson River Valley and Southern Mountains

Above
Yellow iris are in full bloom along the Foundry Park shore-line at Cold Spring. This area is the northern perimeter of Audubon's Constitution Marsh Sanctuary on the east bank of the Hudson River.

Left
Wild azaleas have just started blooming on this beautiful late spring day at the Sunset Rock overlook in Catskill Park.

THE HUDSON RIVER is really an arm of the sea. It is also the only navigable waterway on our East Coast that penetrates the barrier of the Appalachian Mountains. Traveling the Hudson is like watching one of the grand artistic parchment panoramas of old scrolling by. How well I remember as a child riding the New York Central Railroad north from New York City along the Hudson, pulled by a monstrous, breathing steam locomotive with driving wheels taller than I was. The New York Central conductor called out, "Peekskill, Peekskill next stop, Peekskill!" naming place after place as we rolled along the mighty river—Peekskill, Newburgh, Poughkeepsie, Kingston, Hudson, Albany—places fixed in American history.

Always, the river was next to me on the left. To my right contained by the tracks were pools and marshes, cattails and ducks, the train a chuffing, giant spider racing along its strand of web stretching ahead and behind. At Albany, the railroad bore west along the Mohawk. We got off at Fonda, then traveled by auto over the hills to grandmother's house.

All along its length, the river is the defining element. The Catskill and Shawangunk mountain ranges are to its west, the Taconics to the east. The river bisects granite hills—the Hudson Highlands between Peekskill and Newburgh—and helps define the Blue Ridge Mountains to the south and the Berkshires and Green Mountains to the north and east.

The Hudson is tidal all the way to Troy, 154 miles from the river's mouth at New York City, and home to creatures from the ocean. Imagine seeing at Staatsburg, eighty miles north of New York City, fish that can live sixty years and grow to fourteen feet—Atlantic sturgeon. In 1992, biologists with the Fish and Wildlife Service netted adult Atlantic sturgeon at Staatsburg and started a captive breeding program; the Hudson River has the largest reproducing population of these fish on the East Coast. Today, fishing for them is banned as the species tries to recover from a population of fewer than one thousand adults, down from a high of around fourteen thousand in the late 1800s.

On the river, about twenty-five miles below Staatsburg, is Constitution Marsh Sanctuary, maintained by the Audubon Society. Here, where the Appalachian Mountains and this arm of the Atlantic meet in a narrowing of the river, the brackish mix of fresh and salt waters created by the tides combines habitats—white-tailed deer flicking their tails and poisonous copperheads sunning on rocks are within a stone's throw of saltwater crustaceans.

Below the sanctuary, the narrow Hudson played an important part in America's historic struggle for independence—at a time when the intersection was of different ideologies rather than different ecologies. Twice, American revolutionaries strung chains across the Hudson in an attempt to forestall the British advance along this vital waterway. In 1777, the colonists extended a chained boom across the river at Bear Mountain near Peekskill. Sir Henry Clinton destroyed that one for the British.

Two otters rest on some rocks near the edge of Lake Tiorati in Harriman State Park. One dines on a fish while the other hangs around hoping to scrounge for scraps.

Sunlight filters through an isolated pine and reflects off the Hudson River's broad Tappan Zee at the edge of a palisade at Hook Mountain State Park, north of Nyack.

The next chain was put across in the spring of 1778 and was much more substantial. Having eight hundred two-foot links—weighing about 125 pounds each—forged at the Sterling Furnace in the Ramapo Mountains just to the west, this chain was supported in the water by about forty huge log rafts. No Royal British Navy warships tried to breast the chain. By blocking the river and its valley, the British offensive was effectively kept out of the Northeast during the Revolutionary War. Almost one-third of Revolutionary War battles were fought on or near the Hudson River.

A century and a half later, Bear Mountain was appreciated more for its natural beauty than its strategic military placement, and in 1923 it became the start of the first stretch of the Appalachian Trail, heading south to the Delaware Water Gap.

The early light of a hazy fall morning illuminates the mountains of the Catskill Forest Preserve, as viewed from the summit of Black Dome.

Today, the deep channel below the mountain is the major spawning area for Hudson River striped bass.

Bear Mountain is located in the Hudson Highlands, the heart of the Hudson Valley. The Highlands are a roughly fifteen-mile stretch between Peekskill to the south and Newburgh to the north. Hills loom more than one thousand feet high along both banks. In addition to the river's mix of fresh and brackish waters here, the area marks a divide between northern and southern ecosystems of the eastern woodlands. North-facing slopes harbor Canada and Blackburnian warblers, and other northern birds are near the southern limits of their ranges, as are tundra bog moss and subarctic black spruce. Pushing the northern limits of their ranges are turkey vultures, cardinals, and mockingbirds, which in George Washington's time came only as far north as Washington, D.C., until the introduction of the multiflora rose by mankind encouraged extension of the birds' range.

By the early 1900s, the Hudson Highlands had begun to lose much of their beauty to development. An attempt by the State of New York to relocate the infamous Sing Sing Prison to Bear Mountain triggered an organized effort to protect the lands from further encroachment. Hoping to block the move, Union Pacific president E. W. Harriman and other well-to-do businessmen with homes in the area donated land and money to purchase additional property for a forest preserve. The result was the formation of Bear Mountain–Harriman State Park, in 1910. On a clear day, the Manhattan skyline is visible forty-five miles to the south.

North of Bear Mountain is the United States Military Academy at West Point, and adjoining West Point to the north is Storm King State Park. The controversy over Storm King Mountain that began in 1962—a battle that lasted for seventeen years—helped to launch modern environmental activism. The state's major power and electric company, Con Edison, wanted to build a huge hydroelectric plant on the Hudson near Cornwall. The eventual victory for local residents and conservation advocates was rooted in the U.S. Court of Appeals' reasoning that protection of natural resources was as important as economic gain. The Storm King case led Congress to pass the National Environmental Policy Act of 1969, which mandated that an environmental-impact study be done on any major project requiring federal governmental approval.

Another important outgrowth of the Storm King Mountain controversy was the formation of Clearwater—an organization founded by folk musician/activist Pete Seeger to advocate for protection of the Hudson River and other waterways—and the creation of the group's eponymous wooden sloop sailing the Hudson in the interest of the river's protection. Today, the independent environmental advocacy group Riverkeeper monitors the Hudson's ecological integrity and reports companies that dump illegally.

Northwest of the Highlands, and still within a two-hour drive of New York City, Catskill Park is a huge area of public and privately owned land sprawling through the ancient mountains and lush forests of Ulster, Greene, Delaware, and Sullivan counties. About 40 percent of the park's 700,000-plus acres is state owned and forms the Catskill Forest Preserve. An 1894 amendment to the state constitution designated the state-owned land as Forever Wild, similar to the protection granted to public lands in the Adirondacks, ensuring that it would never be sold off, managed, or otherwise developed or the timber sold.

Even before constitutional protections were instituted, the Catskills' steepest mountainsides and deepest valleys kept at bay the industries of logging, charcoal production, and tanbark harvesting, leaving today's old-growth hemlock and northern hardwood forests. Those tanneries that once existed here supplied most of the saddles used in the Civil War, using bark from hemlocks to tan the hides.

Although some of the creeks, in the words of journalist Michael Hill, are said to "run like Yoo-hoo after heavy rains," the forest preserve today contains the remains of old farmsteads and hundreds of miles of abandoned woods roads. The park is also rich with wildlife worthy of respect, including bears—there are about four hundred in the area—and rattlesnakes.

The beauty of the region has also inspired many great scribes. Washington Irving set his 1819 tale of *Rip Van Winkle* in the Catskills, and James Fennimore Cooper's fictional Natty Bumpo referred to the very real Kaaterskill Falls as "the best piece of work I've met with in the woods; and none know how often the hand of God is seen in the wilderness, but them that rove it for a man's life."

The Catskills have been called "America's First Wilderness" by some scholars

A variety of millipede found only in old-growth forests clambers over the bark of one of the largest pines growing in the Mianus River Gorge Preserve.

Kaaterskill Falls in the Catskill Mountains has been inspiring writers and nature lovers for generations.

who assign the beginnings of the environmental conservation movement to the area. Although the Adirondacks, in 1892, were the first to be granted park status—a designation not extended to the Catskills until a dozen years later—parts of both the Adirondacks and the Catskills attained forest preserve status in 1885. To be sure, the Catskills' proximity to New York City brought it widespread attention earlier.

While the Catskillians and Adirondackers might quibble over which park rightly deserves credit as the true origin of the environmental movement, the Mianus River Gorge in Westchester County can, with less dispute, lay claim as the birthplace of direct-action conservation by The Nature Conservancy. Two years after the Conservancy was formed in 1951, a group from the town of Bedford approached the organization about protecting the gorge from development. The Mianus River Gorge Conservation Committee encouraged the Conservancy to purchase some sixty acres in its pioneer land-preservation project. The Mianus River Gorge Preserve now spreads over more than 700 acres, 555 of which are owned by The Nature Conservancy.

Near Bedford today, the gorge boasts a hemlock cathedral with trees over 325 years old, trees saved again by their inaccessibility to human interference. The gorge's moist and cool microclimate supports a hemlock-northern hardwood forest usually only found farther north. Such forests are home to not only the eastern hemlock, but also sugar and red maples, American beech, and yellow birch. In the understory are hay-scented fern, bracken, club moss, and bunchberry, or dwarf dogwood, with its bright red-orange berries.

Some environmental protection efforts are more fun than, say, lawyering it out with Con Ed. Beginning in the late 1980s, activists and locals concerned with the Susquehanna River have been getting together for weeklong canoe trips on the river. In addition to paddling and camping, these "Susquehanna Sojourns" host educational programs and meetings with elected officials to discuss the importance of protecting the river and its watershed.

The 444-mile-long North Branch of the Susquehanna has its origin at Otsego Lake (the "Glimmerglass" of James Fennimore Cooper's *Leatherstocking Tales*) near Cooperstown, New York, and, with the West Branch in Pennsylvania and other tributaries, the Susquehanna contributes one-half of the freshwater flow to the Chesapeake Bay. The river drains an area almost the size of South Carolina and forms a watershed spread over New York, Pennsylvania, and Maryland.

While the Susquehanna's imprint is hard to miss, some of the region's other natural attractions require looking underground. Howe Caverns, a private enterprise off I-88 west of Albany, bills itself as the second most visited natural attraction in New York State, after Niagara Falls.

The caverns were discovered by Lester Howe in the summer of 1842 when he saw his cows—the story has it the instrumental cow was named Millicent—cooling themselves in the air coming out of a cave entrance Howe didn't know was there.

The caves (which were upgraded to "caverns" when a closed-stock corporation formed in 1927) feature hundreds of stalactites and stalagmites formed a drop at a time by limestone-laden water. On the walls is flowstone, another type of limestone deposit resembling ice. The cave maintains a constant temperature of 52 degrees Fahrenheit.

That it took a cow to find the caves suggests other natural surprises are still to be found, either by us or with help from fellow creatures. Perhaps not everything in Nature has been discovered yet.

Below, top
Skunk cabbage thrives in a wet area along the trail that parallels the Mianus River in the upper part of The Nature Conservancy's first preserve.

Below, bottom
The Henry Morgenthau Preserve, another Nature Conservancy property, offers trails through hardwood forest near the shores of Blue Heron Lake in Westchester County.

Facing page
Glowing in the afternoon sun, the foliage of blueberry bushes turns a brilliant red in the fall. This view looks south over Bear Mountain State Park from the overlook on Bear Mountain.

Left
Towering oak trees provide a colorful autumn canopy near Stillman Spring at Storm King State Park on the Hudson River.

Below
Lake Tiorati is one of many serene settings to be encountered along Seven Lakes Parkway in Harriman State Park.

Left
Viewed from the top of Popolopen Torne, Bear Mountain State Park is a densely treed and lush rolling landscape in the Hudson Highlands.

Below
A panoramic view looking north up the Hudson River from Storm King State Park toward Breakneck Ridge and the town of Newburgh.

Above
The conglomerate rock found on this outcropping on the summit of Schunnemunk Mountain is from the same strata as is found on the tops of some of the Catskill Mountains. The 1,664-foot Schunnemunk Mountain forms the western boundary of the Hudson Highlands.

Right
Canada geese rest in the calm waters of a bend on the Upper Delaware Scenic and Recreational River near the Long Eddy and Basket areas on the Pennsylvania border. The first 73.4 miles of the 331-mile-long Delaware River are federally protected as a National Wild and Scenic River.

Above, top
Oak trees gracefully arch over a wetland flow in the Neversink Preserve. This 550-acre area in Orange County is managed by The Nature Conservancy to protect the diverse ecosystem of the Neversink River.

Above, bottom
A young porcupine—quills at attention—scurries up a large oak tree at the Neversink Preserve.

Above
Ferns grow in abundance under the shelter of some oaks in a moist area along the trail to Verkeerder Kill Falls in the Sam's Point Dwarf Pine Preserve. The preserve is protected by the Open Space Institute in cooperation with The Nature Conservancy.

Above

This 360-degree panoramic view from Sunset Rock in Catskill Park looks down on North-South Lake and the eastern escarpment of the Catskills.

Right

Sam's Point Dwarf Pine Preserve, in the Shawangunk Mountains, is one of the world's best examples of a ridge-top dwarf pine barrens. The view from the old fire-tower site at High Point looks across the Rondout Creek Valley toward the Catskill Mountains.

Left
In wintertime, Hunter Mountain is one of the most popular ski areas in New York State. In autumn, the trees take center stage with their colorful foliage.

This beautiful cascade on Kaaterskill Creek is along Route 23A at the trailhead for Kaaterskill Falls.

Above
Seemingly frozen in time, Kaaterskill Falls is an ice-climber's paradise on a cold winter's day.

Left
At 260 feet, Kaaterskill Falls is the second highest waterfall in the state. Illuminated by the midday sun, it's easy to see why James Fenimore Cooper called it "the best piece of work I've met with in the woods."

Above

The Albany Pine Bush Preserve harbors patches of lupines—food for the endangered Karner blue butterfly. Here a tiger swallowtail butterfly enjoys some of the nectar. The Nature Conservancy calls the preserve "a living museum of our natural heritage."

Facing page

The older pitch pines standing in burn areas of the Albany Pine Bush Preserve bear a slightly charcoaled bark. Red oak and blueberries dominate much of the scrub growth. The Nature Conservancy maintains the preserve with prescribed burns to help perpetuate the natural process. Fire is needed to release seeds from the pitch pine cones and to keep the oaks from dominating the pine barrens.

Above
The waters of the Mohawk River rush over Cohoes Falls in a torrent during the spring high water. Before the Erie Canal opened up western New York's Niagara Falls to tourists, Cohoes Falls was the state's most prominent cascade.

Facing page
The reeds along the shoreline at the Thompson Pond Preserve at the foot of Stissing Mountain temporarily obscure a flock of resting Canada geese. The preserve was designated a National Natural Landmark in 1973 and is protected by The Nature Conservancy as a prime example of a calcareous wetland.

"Mountains are the beginning and the end of all natural scenery; in them, and in the forms of inferior landscape that lead to them, my affections are wholly bound up."
—John Ruskin, 1888

Chapter 2

HEAVEN CAUGHT BETWEEN MOUNTAINS AND SKY

THE ADIRONDACKS AND TUG HILL PLATEAU

Above
An antler drop lies atop a cliff on Treadway Mountain, overlooking Pharaoh Lake and some of the Adirondacks' more gentle southern foothills.

Left
Only the highest peaks stand above the clouds on this late winter morning, viewed from the summit of Noonmark Mountain. The Green Mountains of Vermont are visible on the distant horizon.

IN THE MIDDLE of May in the heart of the Adirondacks, I was sitting alone at the Cold River lean-to on one of the first hot days of the year. I had canoed up to Raquette Falls, a mile-long rapids on the Raquette River on its way to the St. Lawrence, then walked through the woods to the lean-to.

I rested on the deacon's bench, the great sill log that is the lean-to's front seat. I hadn't been here in over twenty-five years. Some things were different: The outside table was now fastened on the other side of the lean-to. The fireplace, like almost all those at lean-tos in the Adirondacks, was a quasi-jumble of rocks, a candidate for a trowel and forty pounds of mortar cement. Somebody ought to do it, I thought, ducking personal consideration of the task.

In front of me, pistachio shells were scattered near but not into the fireplace. Somebody probably meant well, but his or her aim or arm power was lacking. The lean-to was otherwise swept clean; a broom stood inside and a leaf rake hung on the outer south wall. Unable to ignore the pistachio shells any longer, I took the rake and herded the shells into the stone fireplace.

I sat in the sun and made some notes, incapable of writing without clichés. For indeed the air was *redolent* with the odors of green balsam and old pine needles marinating in the sun-baked dirt. The trees and duff, that aged compost of many autumns' leaves and branches, were *exuding* a sweet and earthy scent. In my notes

Snow dusts the fall foliage and the loftier High Peaks elevations in this view across South Meadow toward Mount Marcy, Mount Colden, and Algonquin Peak from the summit of Mount Van Hoevenberg.

couldn't they merely *smell nice?* No. No more than could the first sunny days back in April that triggered the *pungent exudates* of conifers.

For not until mid-April, and the smells and the cacophonous spring peepers, will you really begin to believe spring is here. The peepers' chorus—contrapuntal, discordant, chaotic, and glorious—coupled with smells that have been missing for five months mean that *eternal winter* is trying to leave, fitfully. Hope returns along with thoughts in italics. I cherish the *crystal days* of spring and summer even more than the *crystal days* of winter, perhaps because there are fewer of them.

Arguably still the best all-around book on the Adirondacks is William Chapman White's *Adirondack Country*, which came out originally in 1954 and has had some short updates. In his chapter "Adirondack Year," he writes:

> In earliest May the Adirondack world is one of delicate color. Maples show a pale red-scarlet, birches a light green. Tamarack are palest yellow. At a distance the woods seem washed with lilac in some lights, with rose-pink and mauve in others. Even the sunsets take on a fresh brightness. Leafing-out is slow, although warm rain and hot sun can hurry it so that in some years it seems to happen overnight. Places that were sunny in the winter have fresh new shade. Long vistas in the woods are closed off by bright green walls. . . . On some days summer seems to have come for good: the next day is chill and the night brings frost. . . . On the distant hills the summits stay snow-capped until well on in the month. . . . On the high peaks dwarfed trees try for new growth and little Alpine flowers bloom at the edge of the snow.

Rime frost and snow cover the trees near timberline on the Giant Ridge trail. The trail traverses a rocky open section of the ridge on the way to the summit of Giant Mountain.

Ten or twelve thousand years earlier, White would have seen a very different landscape, of course, as the whole area was covered by a receding glacier. During the glacier's retreat, not on little cat feet but with awful scrapings and groans and echoing booms, boulders called erratics were scattered here and there, and its underground rivers deposited serpentine ridges visible today as sandy eskers, home to red pine and lady's slippers.

The Adirondacks' greatest geologic legacy is its mountains. The original survey of the range counted forty-six peaks above four thousand feet, although four of the peaks have since been "downgraded" a few hundred feet short of the four-thousand-foot plateau. Nevertheless, climb all forty-six peaks—even those that measure in at only 3,800 feet—and you are eligible to become a "46er," a group with an almost religious reverence for the mountains.

Peter Hackett, a physician and world-class mountain climber, conveys well his own reverence for mountains: "My bias is that there is something inherent in people that makes them feel better and more centered in the mountains than in other places." The Adirondacks' 130,000 or so permanent residents agree, sometimes grudgingly, with that bias.

Joined "at the hips" between the Adirondack Park to the east and Lake Ontario to the west is an area with almost no resident population and no roads through its heart. The Tug Hill Plateau, made up of parts of Oswego, Jefferson, Lewis, and Oneida counties, covers approximately 160,000 acres, much of it northern hardwood forest. It receives an annual snowfall of fifteen to twenty feet, more than any other area in New York State.

Less well known than the Adirondacks, the Tug Hill Plateau nevertheless has its own attractions, including four state wildlife management areas. To the west on the plateau, the Happy Valley Wildlife Management Area near Parish is geologically part of the Ontario lowlands, distinguished by low ridges and swamplands. Further north also on the western edge of Tug Hill, as the area is familiarly called, is the Littlejohn Wildlife Management Area, consisting of over eight thousand completely forested acres. That acreage converts to 750 square miles of dense forest, mostly maple, with bobcats, black bear, fishers (a fox-like member of the marten family), goshawks, and blackburnian warblers—but no houses.

Sitting at an elevation of 1,400 feet, Littlejohn is flat, the kind of flatness that translates to a plateau. But it does rise, imperceptibly, away from Lake Ontario. The plateau rises gradually to more than two thousand feet on its eastern edge as it approaches the Adirondacks, and it contains gorges up to two hundred feet deep.

Tug Hill's gorges are the legacy of four glacial ages, beginning nearly two million years ago during the Pleistocene era and ending about ten thousand years ago, when the last ice sheet melted away. As the glaciers advanced across the land, they smoothed hilltops and dug out valleys. On their retreat, the ice melted into fast-running rivers that further scoured the valleys. Boonville Gorge, on the eastern side of Tug Hill near Buck Hill State Forest, is a prime example of these powerful geological forces.

As you might expect, an untrammeled area of this size is a source of water for communities on its borders. Tagasoke Reservoir, created in 1960 by the damming of Fish Creek, provides drinking water for Rome and Oneida, two cities near the New York Thruway; the east branch of Fish Creek also supplies drinking water to Rome.

Even long after the glaciers left, the inhospitable climate discouraged year-round settlement in the central Adirondacks and most of Tug Hill until about 1800. The ubiquitous great forest in and around the mountains provided the primary material for shelter, tools, and fuel; the animals of the forest were the basic food source. The Indians saw their connection to all this; to them, mankind was just one more interdependent piece of the natural order. Those connections changed with the coming of the Europeans, even though the newcomers, as subsistence farmers, were reliant on the land's offerings.

Earlier and to the east, on the other side of the Adirondacks from Tug Hill, occurred one of those quirky historical coincidences that seem to happen fairly frequently. In the same year—1609—Henry Hudson came up the river that now bears

Canada geese rest during the fall migration on a farm pond near Martinsburg in the northern Tug Hill Plateau.

his name, and Samuel de Champlain down the lake later named after him. (The river and lake were eventually joined by a canal.) Probably not much more than one hundred miles apart, they didn't encounter each other. Sporting firearms and exploring for the French—and apparently egged on by Algonquin Indians in what is now French Canada—Champlain battled the Mohawks of the Iroquois Nation near Crown Point (some historians say it was near Ticonderoga).

The reductionist version of the outcome of this battle is that forevermore the Mohawks allied themselves with the British instead of the French; in fact, the story of Indian alliances is more convoluted than that. But during the French and Indian Wars of the mid-eighteenth century, which pitted the French and their Indian allies against the British and their Indian allies, the Mohawks indeed sided with the British. (Any socio-algebraic equation will show that some Indians had to be among the losers.)

Soon after the end of the Revolutionary War, the newly independent and cash-strapped state of New York sold off huge tracts of Adirondack and former Mohawk lands for pennies an acre to speculators, most of whom never came. The Mohawks were shunted onto reservations and marginalized.

The early and middle nineteenth century saw widespread logging across the region. Thousands of logs, virtually the only cash crop, were floated to the edges of the area, particularly down the Hudson River. The heavy logging of the landscape, however, allowed water to run off too rapidly, undermining the stability of a watershed for New York City, especially, and water for feeder streams for canals to the south. This led to an effort to re-create wildness and some of the first state-protected lands in the nation. While aesthetic considerations may be what draw most visitors to the Adirondacks today, those issues were secondary to the more practical concerns of potable drinking water and commerce in the late nineteenth century.

In 1885 the state of New York formed the Forest Commission to protect a core quarter of a million acres of state-owned land in the Adirondacks. As land speculators continued to log their private lands and then default on the taxes after the trees were cut, the state gradually accumulated even more land.

In 1892 the state created the Adirondack Park, a mix of public and private land today totaling about six million acres; in 1894 the state-owned lands were given constitutional protection. As part of the forest preserve, the lands are to be kept Forever Wild, not managed or sold.

Adirondack forests range from Lake Champlain's near sea level to Mount Marcy's summit more than 5,300 feet above the lake. The tree species change with elevation in fairly well-defined strata: red oak populates the lowlands; balsam,

Pink lady's slippers bloom in May on the shore of Lake George's Northwest Bay.

tamarack, ash, cedar, and yellow birch flourish at 1,500 to 2,000 feet. Going higher still, above the hardwoods, are spruce and hemlock. Mount Marcy's peak is above tree line; the balsams here are stunted and crooked, a hundred growth rings crowd into a trunk a few inches in diameter. This zone accommodates a true arctic or alpine flora, harboring Lapland rosebay and *Diapensia lapponica*, which has no common name; those familiar with the pretty flower know it as just *diapensia*.

Nearly as varied as the Adirondacks' flora are its lakes and ponds, of which there are about 2,500. There is little rhyme or reason as to what is a pond and what is a lake. Numerous ponds and lakes abound named Mud or Long or Lost. Local boundaries add to the confusion: The village of Saranac Lake, for example, is in two counties and three townships. The village is on Lake Flower, named for a former governor; Upper, Middle (also known as Round), and Lower Saranac lakes are various distances away.

To get across bodies of Adirondack water, one of the most ingenious watercraft in the world was devised here: the Adirondack guideboat. The first hunters and trappers who came to the area early in the nineteenth century realized that they needed a type of boat that could be carried from lake to lake (or pond to lake, pond to pond, and so on). The retreated glacier had scoured out many stream and river valleys, some with abundant watercourses between them but others with mere trickles or only dry land connecting them.

A guideboat is made from indigenous materials using European boat-building techniques. The heart and strength of the boat is its spruce ribs. You make small, finger-thick ribs from blanks (slabs two to three inches thick) cut where the trunk tapers into the roots. The grain of the wood follows that taper, giving great strength to the ribs. The result is a rowing boat of astonishing speed and beauty, weighing about seventy-five pounds. Many an Adirondacker will tell you that his or her life is complete with a guideboat, a pick-up truck, and a sharp axe. All else is dross.

For me, the Adirondacks' moods are most apparent on her waters—here her emotions are worn on her sleeve. The most evident expression of emotion is created by the wind. A strong wind, perhaps coming from the south and curling whitecaps, suddenly shifts. Coming now from the west, it drops in an instant, the water now mere ripples.

A sailor in a small boat despairs at the fluky, changeable winds and tries futilely to sail ashore. The performance is right out of a Charlie Chaplin movie. On a dock near shore, onlookers see the fecklessly flapping sails and debate whether to row or motor out and tow the hapless sailor in. (This happened to Albert Einstein more than once on Lake Flower in the village of Saranac Lake.)

In the summer, sailors and watchers alike are "in camp." Camps range from shacks to mansions, but the buildings themselves are secondary. What matters is what "in camp" means. Clocks and time count for nothing. Newspapers go unread, or started and abandoned. The rising and setting sun dictates sleep and meals. Sitting on a deck or porch watching the pond seems the only thing worth doing.

A small tributary to the Lansing Kill cascades over numerous ledges as it flows toward the base of Pixley Falls, located in the southeastern corner of Tug Hill.

"Look!" someone says, "A pair of loons! Are they the same ones that were here last summer, or maybe their offspring? Do they have a nest on the pond?"

Watching the pond tells us what we have lost—quiet. Nature is, of course, hardly ever quiet, with her winds and creatures and rustlings. But somehow we don't think of that as noise. Watching the pond, a wonderful lassitude can overcome you, an odd, comfortable exhaustion from doing nothing. The sensation is of stress draining out through your fingertips, the true, free you emerging.

For the most part, the constitutional protection of the Adirondack Forest Preserve has been a godsend for the park, the people of New York, and park visitors from around the world—albeit not without controversy. For example, in recent years, a variety of organizations have proposed and even initiated the reintroduction of extirpated, indigenous species of wildlife that would not be welcomed by some residents. ("Extirpated" might be inexactly defined as extinct in a given region, but still existing elsewhere.) Among these are the Canada lynx, eastern mountain lion, moose, and the gray wolf.

The howl of the wolf is thought by wildlife advocates today to rank up there with the call of the loon as a defining wilderness sound. Both sounds (along with the snuffle of a nearby bear or the screech-hiss of an "attacking" mother grouse) can toy with the hair on the back of your neck.

The gray wolf, hunted to near extinction in the continental United States in the 1930s, had been eliminated, or extirpated, from the Adirondacks by about 1890. Coyotes, accomplished howlers in their own right, gradually took over the wolves' ecological niche, and New York has been more or less coyote country since the wolves have been gone. While many people argue that wolves are greater threats to humans and livestock than coyotes are, some of those working for reintroduction say wolves are good for the Adirondack ecosystem, that they are more effective predators than coyotes and will move deer around a given area, which in turn benefits plant species and thus benefits smaller animals.

For now it looks like the wolves will have to wander back on their own, if at all. The mere prospect of their return makes the region seem even wilder.

Above
A loon rests on her nest on Little Clear Pond in the northern Adirondacks.

Below
Canoeing Lake Lila at sunset is a particularly serene way to enjoy the Adirondack's many waterways.

Mountain sandwort and sedges thrive in protected pockets on the alpine summits of the highest peaks in the Adirondacks. This view from Algonquin Peak—the second highest summit in New York state, at 5,114 feet—looks toward Iroquois Peak and the early morning fog in the valleys to the south.

Left
Known as Ulloa's rings or the Spectre of the Brocken, this atmospheric apparition appears when the sun shines brightly behind you with the mountain mist in front of you. Mount Marcy is to the right in this view from Algonquin Peak.

Below
A red eft makes his way to the summit marker on Algonquin Peak. This species of newt begins life in the water and then lives on land for two to three years before returning to live underwater again. Generally an inhabitant of lower elevations, perhaps this adventurous creature was bagging peaks.

An early snow adds a touch of white to autumn's rich reds and yellows, like icing on a colorful cake. This view from Mount Jo looks down to Heart Lake and to Algonquin Peak, in the clouds on the right.

Below
A partial rainbow forms over the High Peaks following a summer shower. The rugged High Peaks are the heart of the Adirondack Mountains, with Mount Marcy (*center*) topping all the other peaks at an elevation of 5,344 feet.

A porcupine looks for a safe place to sleep for the day in an oak tree on Rattlesnake Mountain in the northeastern Adirondacks.

Above

Wild roses grow in the rock crevices along the shoreline of the Hudson River in Warren County Park just north of Warrensburg.

Right

The crystal-clear waters of the Opalescent River drop through this flume along the southern trail to Mount Marcy. The river flows from Lake Tear of the Clouds, the highest source of the Hudson River.

The full moon is just peeking out from behind the ridgeline beyond the Narrows of Lake George. Black Mountain is the peak on the left.

Above
Sporadic fall colors accentuate the shoreline of this wild kettlehole bog in the southeastern Adirondacks. Many similar bogs, with a boreal growth of cotton grass, sundews, pitcher plants, and various orchids, can be found throughout the northern mountains.

Right
As the sun rises above the horizon, the fall colors and the waters of Lake George are briefly highlighted by the dramatic morning light, just before the clouds roll in.

Above
On a cold December morning, freshly formed ice floats along the surface of the Boreas River. By early January, the river will be totally covered with ice.

Left
Round Lake was part of a 26,500-acre Adirondack Nature Conservancy project that protected numerous ponds, wetlands, and forest lands in the Little Tupper Lake area.

Right

A newborn fawn, no larger than a large house cat, rests in the fallen leaves and young maples on the forest floor. Since they have no scent when they are young, they are safe from predators while the mother goes elsewhere to feed.

Below

Wood sorrel blooms in July on the forest floor of Buck Island on the southern portion of Lake Lila.

Left
A pair of Canada geese float through the morning fog on the Raquette River near Tupper Lake.

Below
The first light of day casts a beautiful pastel hue across the waters of Lake Champlain, as seen from the Ausable Point Campground area. The Green Mountains of Vermont are on the horizon.

Above

A mother blue heron—on the right—tries to feed her nearly full-grown offspring in their nest high in an old pine tree at a blue heron rookery in the southeastern Adirondacks.

Right

Lyon Mountain is the centerpiece of the Sable Highlands. In early 2005, the Adirondack Nature Conservancy completed negotiations to protect more than 104,000 acres of wild timberlands and wetlands in the northern Adirondacks through outright purchase and conservation easements. This view looks across to Ellenburg Mountain and Chazy Lake.

Above
The sheer cliff walls in the upper reaches of Whetstone Gulf State Park are a dramatic sight when covered with snow in winter. The Tug Hill Plateau receives the most annual snowfall of any area east of the Rocky Mountains, due to the lake effect snows blowing in from Lake Ontario.

Left
Lily pads cover an old beaver flow along Little John Drive in the Tug Hill Plateau.

"*What voices spoke from out the thundering water; . . . what Heavenly promise glistened in those angels' tears, the drops of many hues, that showered around, and twined themselves about the gorgeous arches which the changing rainbows made!*"
—Charles Dickens, 1842

Chapter 3

JOINING THE WATERS

NIAGARA FALLS, TWO GREAT LAKES, AND A RUN FOR THE SEA

Above
Weather-beaten roots hold back the collection of small cobbles and skipping stones that make up the Scotts Bluffs shoreline.

Left
A storm-battered stump clings to a rock along Lake Ontario's southeastern shoreline at Scotts Bluff. The rounded rock to the left of the stump features fossil imprints.

New York City might wish in vain for Niagara Falls with all its spectacularity. Over Times Square, say, spotlights could drive patriotic red, white, and blue through the upwardly curling mist of that magnificent cataract. Nothing else in the Big Apple would come close.

But it is not to be, for Niagara Falls is decidedly a defining natural landmark of western New York. Bracketing the state in much the way that the manmade Montauk Point lighthouse does on the eastern tip of Long Island, it forces New York City and all points in between to find some other way to make their mark.

The falls are part of the Niagara River, which flows out of Lake Erie at Buffalo on its approximately twenty-seven-mile journey north to Lake Ontario. The international boundary between Canada and the United States is in the middle of the river below the falls.

Niagara Falls and nearby Buffalo were little known to most New York City dwellers until about 1825, when the Erie Canal connected the Hudson River to Lake Erie. Until then, western New York had kept her natural secrets to herself, hidden to all except a few pioneer settlers and, before them, Native Americans, followed by feuding French and English.

With the opening of the canal, however, Niagara Falls quickly became a showy stop on the American Grand Tour of the middle nineteenth century. In addition to the falls, the tour included the Hudson River, the Catskills, Lake George, the Erie Canal, the White Mountains, and the Connecticut Valley. Our young country's bold natural attractions took the place of Europe's cathedrals and monuments. New York State held the bulk of the required stops.

Charles Dickens stopped at the falls on his own "grand tour" of America in 1842. In the face of the roar and raw power of Niagara Falls, he commented: "I felt how near to my Creator I was standing, the first effect, and the enduring one—instant and lasting—of the tremendous spectacle, was Peace."

By the 1860s, the falls had become a victim of commercialization, as well as political pressures to use the water power for industrialization. The artist Frederic Church and the landscape architect Frederick Law Olmsted, designer of Central Park, proposed that the state establish a park at Niagara Falls. In 1887, Olmsted and his colleague Calvert Vaux submitted their final plan, and so creation of the nation's first state park partly restricted commercial development of the falls.

Earlier, in 1868, the peripatetic Olmsted and Vaux had begun creation of six parks in nearby Buffalo. Their parks system, instituted over about thirty years, was probably the first of its kind in the nation, and it makes up 75 percent of the city's parkland today. Olmsted called Delaware Park, one of his first three parks, simply "The Park," and its 350 acres serve as Buffalo's version of Central Park in Manhattan. Another of the original three, Front Park, is situated on a bluff overlooking the Niagara River and Lake Erie. Olmsted thought of Front Park as showcasing Buffalo's "public face."

Facing page
Spectacular Niagara Falls has been attracting tourists and nature lovers for centuries. It also fostered a groundbreaking step toward protecting the state's natural wonders.

Tifft Nature Preserve, located just outside of downtown Buffalo, is not part of the park system but is owned by the City of Buffalo and administered by the Buffalo Museum of Science. Its 264 acres contain 75 acres of cattail marsh. There is a boardwalk into the marsh, with muskrat lodges visible. The contrast between Tifft and its surroundings is especially pronounced, as the nearby waterfront holds forlorn sentinels of the rust belt—railyards, ship berths, and grain elevators—giving a special poignancy to a walk in Tifft.

About twenty miles to the southeast, near East Aurora, Hunter Creek County Park features a striking 185-foot gorge. The gorge is not only visually stunning, but climbing up and down it is probably an irresistible challenge to, say, adolescent males. But the shale rock is loose and footings are precarious and dangerous; with no safe trail down into the gorge, it is more prudent to appreciate the view from above.

In the school year of 1999–2000, my wife and I lived near Buffalo while she worked on a master's degree. During that time, we visited Tifft Preserve, Hunter Creek, and some of the area's so-called lesser attractions. I am embarrassed to say we never visited Niagara Falls. Now, the reasons are obscure but include sloth and distractibility. Later, back home in the Adirondacks, we were upbraided by a fervent birdwatcher friend for not going to the falls, missing Bonaparte's gulls, occasional ring-billed gulls, and a colony of black-crowned night-herons nesting on the Dufferin Islands, viewable from shore on the Canadian side of the Niagara River.

Located outside of Buffalo, the Tifft Nature Preserve is a wilderness oasis for people and waterfowl alike, including this pair of Canada geese.

From our rented farm on Sturgeon Point Road in Derby, south of Buffalo, we were drawn almost daily to the shore of Lake Erie. A few miles west of our farm, the road dead-ended into the lake. Just the name Sturgeon Point, seemingly self-explanatory, filled me with curiosity. What was the role of sturgeon in Lake Erie? Were they still there? I couldn't remember what they looked like—all I could think of was some scaly antediluvian creature doing second-rate Loch Ness monster imitations.

Prior to the mid-nineteenth century, lake sturgeon were regarded as trash fish—their flesh and roe had no commercial value. They were dried and burned as fuel, fed to pigs, or used as fertilizer. By 1860, over-fishing and habitat destruction had brought their numbers down to less than one percent of their former numbers. Today, research at the Great Lakes Science Center in Cleveland, Ohio, is helping the sturgeon recover by identifying spawning sites and determining the water quality they need to thrive.

A more appetizing fish can be found in abundance downriver on the Niagara, about twenty-five miles north of Buffalo in Lewiston, the "Smelt Capital of the World." There, night fishermen use long-handled dip nets to scoop up as much as a bushel-basket full of the tasty fish, also called frost fish.

Within an easy bicycle ride of Sturgeon Point, Evangola State Park on Lake Erie offers an arc-shaped shoreline and natural sand beach. Here the shale banks

bordering the shoreline are much less formidable than those in Hunter Creek Park. Nevertheless, park personnel have made an effort to protect us from ourselves. At one spot, they erected a chain-link fence as a safety precaution, guarding a drop of about fifteen feet. This time I can't point any fingers at adolescent males, as I found the little stretch of beach below irresistible. I was able to squirm under the fence, catching my clothes on the pointed wires at the fence bottom. My wife did so, too.

The sun is about to drop below the horizon beyond the undulating frozen waters of Lake Erie at Evangola State Park.

Not far away up the shore on an even higher seventy-foot cliff sits Graycliff, a Frank Lloyd Wright–designed house built between 1926 and 1927. Wright believed in what he called "organic architecture," an attempt to blend his buildings into the natural landscape. One architectural historian noted that Graycliff, with its many windows and breezy layout, was made for "the enjoyment of natural things." Nature is said to have sometimes intruded excessively into Wright houses, such as through roofs that were seemingly designed to leak.

A loop back on our bikes, slightly inland from the lake, brought us to air heavy with the smell of grapes in the fall. Two New York counties bounded by Lake Erie—Chautauqua and Erie—along with the Finger Lakes region to the east share almost 90 percent of the state's vineyard acreage. In fact, those two lakeshore counties have more than half of the total acreage. The vineyards make up the northern half of the Concord grape belt, which borders Lake Erie in New York, Ohio, and Pennsylvania, and where almost 90 percent of the total crop are Concords; almost 100 percent of all the grapes grown are native American varieties. I began to connect

A female snapping turtle performs her annual spring egg-laying ritual in the dunes of the Black Pond State Wildlife Management Area on Lake Ontario.

the names of the varieties—Concord, Niagara, Catawba, Elvira, Delaware—with place names and Native American tribes.

The breezes out of the west blow the aroma of grapes even onto the ridge a couple of miles east of the vineyards. By late fall, the grapes are harvested, the green leaves turned to brown. With the vines in dormancy, the endless task of pruning can begin.

If you bicycle near Buffalo on a fall weekend when the Buffalo Bills are playing football, you can see almost every play by peering through windows at televisions as you go by. A little intrusive, true, but you're not likely to be noticed by the fanatical fans. You have the roads to yourself. The effect is as if people are hunkering down in anticipation of winter.

With the end of autumn we, too, braced for one of those legendary Buffalo winters. The heavy snowfalls from which Buffalo and Erie County get their reputation are the result of lake effect snow. This happens when Arctic air masses flow southward over a relatively warm body of water, in this case Lake Erie. Heat and moisture from the warm lake rise into the Arctic air, where it cools and condenses into snow clouds. The prevailing wind direction dictates where the snow will fall. Even Utah's Great Salt Lake generates lake effect snow.

The lake effect also lends stability and moderation to the climate that grapes welcome. In spring and early summer, the lake water is usually cooler than the air in the daytime, and Lake Erie and Lake Ontario act as natural air conditioners. In addition, the cooler lake waters inhibit the creation of clouds, resulting in more sunny days.

By the end of February, however, we were wondering if the Buffalo brutal-winter hype might be some sort of Chamber of Commerce ploy gone awry. We were riding our bikes again after an unusually tame winter. In fact, Buffalo does not rank the highest in snowfall in western New York. Syracuse, to the east, can claim an average of fifteen more inches a year—108 versus 93.

In the spring, we visited the Iroquois National Wildlife Refuge, northeast of Buffalo, where I hoped to see an eagle. The bald eagle has been a symbol of our country since 1782, when it became part of the Great Seal of the United States. In recent years, the Iroquois Refuge has boasted two pairs on their more than ten thousand acres. One challenge in keeping eagles around is that the young do not stay near the nest after they have flown. In fact, their parents would consider them intruders if they ventured too close. When winter sets in and eagles' diet of mostly fish, small mammals, birds, and snakes is unavailable, the eagles from this region will seek the open waters of the Delaware River, St. Lawrence Seaway, and Great Lakes.

The refuge's wetland habitats are managed with a system of manmade dikes and dams that control water levels on the more than twelve pools and marshes. During the managed dry spells, dead organic materials will decompose and put nutrients into the soil. For a wetland lover like me, the rotten-egg smell from a pool in its water "draw-down" is a welcome odor, a natural by-product of decomposition. Canoeing in marshes, I can conjure up a similar aroma by sticking my paddle in the muck and lifting a little of it up. Most high school chemistry courses have a day devoted to producing a similar stink as well as student revulsion.

The wetland habitats at Iroquois National Wildlife Refuge were restored from parts of the old Oak Orchard Swamp, which had been drained over the last century to create farmland. Pastures for nesting mallards and blue-wing teal are provided by mowing, controlled fire, and grazing and haying agreements with local farmers. The sight of Canada geese and cattle feeding side by side is common.

I didn't see an eagle, but with my low and elastic standards for happiness—a bad day outdoors in nature trumps a good day at the office—I chalked it up as a successful trip anyhow.

If you continue north from the refuge about twenty-five miles, you dead-end at the shore of Lake Ontario. New York has roughly five times as much shoreline on this lake as it does on Lake Erie. Slightly inland from Lake Ontario and running over a hundred miles east and west is Route 104, known as The Ridge. This ridge, formed from gravel pushed up by waves, is virtually continuous from Sodus, east of Rochester, west around the lake to Toronto and beyond. It is the remnant boundary of huge Lake Iroquois, one of the last glacial lakes in eastern America. Present-day Lake Ontario was born from the ancient lake, shaped like Lake Ontario but larger and deeper.

A whitetail deer browses on the fresh spring leaves near a marsh at Tifft Nature Preserve.

The ancient lake contributed to the indigenous architecture by leaving countless cobblestones behind. There are said to be more cobblestone buildings on the twenty-five-mile stretch of the Ridge Road between Rochester and Gaines to the west than on any highway in America. Many masons had come to the region with the building of the Erie Canal in 1825, and the cobblestone style of architecture remained popular until the Civil War.

Collecting enough stones for a house could take three years, and only stones of even shape and color were used. People held "bees" to get together and grade stones. Building the house could take another three years.

Along the shore's edges and into indentations such as Irondequoit Bay near Rochester—one local curmudgeon called that bay "all cattails and green scum"— even the reeds of the cattails were harvested by locals, mostly in the nineteenth century. The stout ones were sold to cooperages to seal beer barrels and thinner ones to cane chairs.

The Indians who lived in the areas along Lake Ontario believed they belonged to their lands as a child belongs to a mother. During the presidency of Martin Van Buren in the late 1830s, however, they lost some of their lands to white speculators and had to buy back some of the tracts.

A trail originally blazed by native tribes later was used to aid fugitive slaves on the Underground Railway in the 1800s. Surely the view north toward Canada was an inspiration for fugitive slaves waiting for a boat and freedom. Decades later, the "cargo" headed the other way across the lake, when rum runners smuggled booze into the United States during Prohibition.

Today, much of the lakeshore consists of summer colonies and numerous state parks, such as Golden Hill, Lakeside Beach, Hamlin Beach, and Selkirk Shores, attracting weekend recreation seekers from Buffalo, Rochester, Syracuse, and places farther afield.

Where Lake Ontario flows northeast into the St. Lawrence River, a sense of intimacy returns. Little Mary Island State Park is just thirteen acres in the Thousand Islands and is reachable only by water. Nearby Wellesley Island State Park is much bigger, at 2,636 acres, and consequently much more populated, but it too offers secluded wilderness spaces for hiking and camping. The Thousand Island region has long been a peaceful refuge for travelers from both sides of the border.

The sandy beaches of Lake Ontario can be as evocative as those of the mighty ocean, if on a much smaller scale.

Back along Lake Erie at the end of our school year in May, we packed up and headed back to the Adirondacks. We were homesick, but still sad to be leaving Lake Erie and our now-familiar bicycle routes. As we pulled out in the stuffed rental truck, one of the kids across the street gave a wistful wave, and I was swept by nostalgia for a place I hadn't even left yet.

We had been little more than tourists during our year in western New York. As Scott Sanders wrote in *Staying Put*, "The work of belonging to a place is never finished. There will always be more to know than any mind or lifetime can hold."

I told my wife I didn't know how or why, but I'd wager that we'd see our farm again within two years. It turned out to be only one. The following year we joined a group of bicycle riders and pedaled from Los Angeles to Boston. When we hit the

This giant, ten-foot-diameter pothole on Wellesley Island is a reminder of the glaciers that once covered the entire region with ice as much as a mile thick. Their abrasive scouring and subsequent melting thousands of years ago created these surface contours.

New York border above Erie, Pennsylvania, I dismounted and kissed the ground. I felt, as Sir Walter Scott wrote, "This is my own, my native land!" I was in my home state, many miles and days from my true home, but just crossing the state boundary was enough.

By then we'd seen about three thousand miles of spectacular country, but I'd already been imprinted by New York. A detour of only a few miles from the day's official route took us past the farm. I wanted to walk back to the pond to see if the old wagon was still there, with its iron-shod wooden wheels sunk into the earth.

Too shy to bother the new tenants, strangers to us, we stood just in the driveway and looked to the back fields. For most of the day we'd sensed and smelled big water and realized we missed Lake Erie.

The kids across the street weren't about, and we had to make it to Hamburg by dusk. We turned and pedaled away from the lake. This time, as we left I made no prediction when we might see Lake Erie and the farm again.

Right

A view upstream in the Niagara Gorge from a talus slope in Devil's Hole State Park. The upper part of the gorge contains the largest series of standing waves of any whitewater in North America, with some waves reaching twelve to eighteen feet high. The Niagara River supports the endangered lake sturgeon, as well as peregrine falcons and bald eagles. In addition, some fourteen species of rare or endangered plants grow within the rugged walls of the gorge.

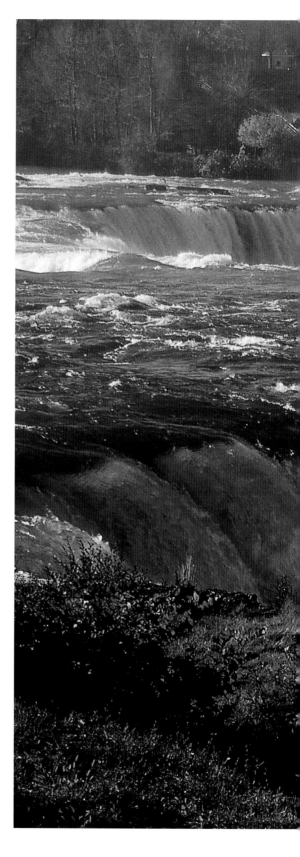

Above

Fractures and weathering of the limestone layer at Devil's Hole State Park creates intriguing patterns in the rock.

Niagara Reservation State Park, created in 1885, is the oldest state park in the United States. The Niagara River is the drainage for four of the five Great Lakes (Superior, Michigan, Huron, and Erie). The waters drop 176 feet from the brim of the falls to the river at the base with a thunderous sound.

Left

Lake Erie State Park is situated on bluffs overlooking the lake's eastern shoreline. Nearly a century of industrial pollution had turned Lake Erie into a virtual marine morgue. Since cleanup began in the 1960s, Erie has been revitalized and is once again a haven for recreation and for migrating waterfowl.

Below

This 360-degree panorama illustrates the striking features of a frozen Lake Ontario at Chimney Bluffs State Park. Heaving waves form contorted ice sculptures along the shore, ice cobbles stretch out on the frozen surface of the lake, and the eroded, badlands-like bluffs catch the light of the setting sun, all below a layer of lake effect clouds extending off into the horizon.

Above

Located on the eastern end of Lake Ontario, the Lakeview Wildlife Management Area features a long sand dune that provides a barrier between the interior lakes and the ravages of the big lake waters. This panorama was taken at the outlet of South Colwell Pond, with the waves of Lake Ontario cresting in the distance.

Right

Like those at the Lakeview area a few miles to the south, the dunes at the Black Pond State Wildlife Management Area shield the inland ponds and shoreline from the effects of the neighboring Great Lake, forming a protected area for migrating and nesting waterfowl and other wildlife.

Above
An abundance of shells and sand cover part of the shoreline at The Nature Conservancy's El Dorado Beach Preserve. This panorama looks over the outlet of Black Pond and out to Lake Ontario on the right.

The Nature Conservancy's Chaumont Barrens is an alvar landscape. This environment—which is characterized by a combination of the extreme conditions of flooding, drought, and poor soil—provides a unique habitat for a variety of plant life. Prairie smoke is one of several prairie plants growing here that cannot be found anywhere else in the northeast.

From Kring Point State Park, the St. Lawrence River appears as a great expanse of water, with islands visible in every direction. These granite islands are a part of the exposed Canadian Shield, which also makes up the Adirondack Mountains. This rock was formed more than one billion years ago and is some of the oldest known rock in the world.

The Thousand Islands support a pleasant mix of northern hardwoods and softwoods. Old willow trees line the moist shorelines of many of the islands, such as these giants gently waving in the breeze on the western edge of Wellesley Island State Park.

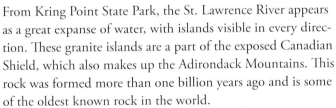

The summer sun sets behind Murray Isle on the St. Lawrence River, viewed from Wellesley Island State Park.

"In nature's infinite book of secrecy, a little I can read."
—William Shakespeare, *Antony and Cleopatra*

Chapter 4

CHAUTAUQUA, ZOAR, AND DEER LICK

THE WESTERN MOUNTAINS AND THE POWER OF PLACE

Above
Chautauqua Creek continues to erode away the layers of soft shale in the bottom of Chautauqua Gorge.

Left
The shale gorge walls rise abruptly from the edge of the rushing water of Cattaraugus Creek in the Zoar Valley.

As you come east and inland from Lake Erie, you enter a part of New York that bears few if any snazzy place names. Not until you get to the Finger Lakes, about sixty miles farther on, do the names resonate elsewhere. But those who live in between don't need any glitzy names. For them, it's all right there.

The year I lived near Buffalo, Zoar Valley was touted to me by a neighbor. "Roar?" I asked, then "Soar?" "No," came the reply, "starts with a Z." His directions were vague, as though the place were a state of mind as much as a natural area. He mentioned as landmarks the towns of Gowanda and Springville. I never found any sort of "this is the main place, start here" site for Zoar Valley, but I found a place of great natural beauty, one I visited numerous times.

Zoar Valley was formed by Cattaraugus Creek, and the valley is the border between Erie and Cattaraugus Counties. One day getting there I turned on a dead-end county road with a stark farm house on the corner. The place appealed to me and suggested an Andrew Wyeth painting, or maybe Hitchcock's *Psycho*—the sort of place that makes you wonder if you really would have enough asocial moxie to make it living there.

At the end of the road, I found a well-worn trail leading to an elevated peninsula that grew narrower and narrower until it reached a point high above the creek, just wide enough for one. The sides of the gorge are so steep that the lumbermen were unable to fell some stands of old growth forest. In the spring, the presence of those trees encourages migrant birds and breeding warblers.

Typical of me, sitting up there on the point, I perversely wanted to be down below in, say, a kayak—with the reverse an obvious given. In the spring, especially, the creek is ready for whitewater boaters. I knew from newspaper accounts that some rafters have had unfortunate experiences there. The words of Scott Sanders in *Staying Put* are chillingly accurate: "Anybody who has not been scared by a river has either not looked at a real one or not looked hard enough."

Descending carefully from the peninsula down to creek level, I came upon what for me is, along with old stone walls, one of the most poignant remnants of human efforts to survive in the wilderness: a stone-walled cellar hole. Human sweat and muscle, perhaps aided by beasts of burden, were pushed to the limit to dig cellar holes and then haul and lay stones for a foundation. A house of logs or boards was built atop the stones, but the house could disappear in a generation or two if neglected, more quickly if the roof was breached. Worse still, the house could be swept away in a flood and disappear in an eye blink, only the cellar stones left behind as mute evidence. This one was so close to the creek, I had to believe it got regularly flooded or maybe even swept away. There was nothing else down there, such as tillable land or the remnants of an orchard, to hint at how the occupants might have made a living. Maybe they couldn't, and abandoned their efforts for another try elsewhere.

On two visits to the area with my wife I met the "Man in Black": black turtleneck and slacks, a Zoar Valley Johnny Cash. I forget his name. It was apparent that

Trillium is in bloom along the pathway leading from Dining Hall Pass, one of the more cavernous passageways among the huge quartz conglomerate rocks at Rock City Park near Olean in southwestern New York.

he spent a lot of time there. Personable, eager to share the area's attractions, he took my wife and me in from an ordinary place on the creek to a waterfall and pool, a spot we would never have found on our own. As Barry Lopez writes in his chapter "The American Geographies" in *Finding Home*:

> To come to an understanding of a specific American geography, requires not only time but a kind of local expertise, an intimacy with place few of us ever develop. There is no way around the former requirement: if you want to know you must take the time. It is not in books. A specific geographical understanding, however, can be sought out and borrowed. It resides with men and women more or less sworn to a place, who abide there, who have a feel for the soil and history, for the turn of the leaves and night sounds. Often they are glad to take the outlander in tow.

Wouldn't it be wonderful if such men, or women, in black were posted to every natural place? You would know when you got there that you should ask them to see—please—the nooks and crannies. You might be asked to take an oath to cherish those places and not reveal them to anyone who wouldn't take a similar oath. "I do solemnly affirm, here in this little glade I never would have known existed. . . ."

French Creek flows south through farmlands before emptying into the Allegheny River on its way to the Mississippi River and, ultimately, the Gulf of Mexico. This tributary is part of the French Creek Watershed managed by The Nature Conservancy.

Sometimes such generous people take farsighted action. One example on the Cattaraugus County side of the valley is Deer Lick Nature Sanctuary. The sanctuary is owned by The Nature Conservancy and managed by its Western New York Chapter. The core of the sanctuary had been a summer campsite called Jordan, owned by the Alverson family. The site was given to the conservancy in 1960, and the following year the adjoining farm was purchased. Three years after that, a man named Herbert Darling deeded almost ninety acres to the project, adding Deer Lick Falls.

The sanctuary was designated a National Landmark in 1967 by the United States Park Service. It now totals 398 acres, a mix of forest—mostly beech, maple, and hemlock—open meadow, and overgrown pastures. This combination of habitats encourages a wide range of plants and animals, including warblers and barred owls.

On a map that shows water as colored blue, Chautauqua Lake, about forty miles southwest of Zoar Valley, looks like one of the Finger Lakes—but a Finger Lake that decided to head west. For while Chautauqua Lake is of a similar size and shape to the others, its north end appears to lean west, straining towards Lake Erie, as if it wants to be a Great Lake when it grows up.

About seventeen miles long, the lake is on a flyway for tundra swans. The swans winter on the Chesapeake Bay and the Outer Banks of North Carolina. In the spring they head for their breeding grounds in the Arctic. In March, as many as a thousand swans might stop on the northern end of Chautauqua Lake.

About ten miles south of the lake's northern tip, early French explorers used an ancient Indian portage trail that ran from what is now Barcelona in far western New York on Lake Erie, past Chautauqua Lake, and continuing into Irvine on the Allegheny River in present Pennsylvania. This forty-mile link, later a wagon and stage coach route, connected the Great Lakes with the Allegheny-Ohio-Mississippi River System, and thus the central and eastern parts of the continent, well in advance of the Erie Canal's completion in 1825.

At about its midpoint, the trail passed below the rock formation known today as Panama Rocks Scenic Park, a privately run natural formation. Panama rocks are sedimentary, put down a layer at a time by an ancient river that contained corals and marine mollusks, traces of which are found today. The accumulated layers created a sort of natural concrete called quartz-conglomerate, forming a ridge that now runs about a half-mile long. Any existing fractures in the rock were widened under the weight of the glacier about ten thousand years ago, leaving hundreds of crevices and passageways. Humans found at least two practical uses for the crevices: Native Americans used the deepest ones, lined with ice well into July, to preserve food; more modern people sought out the warmer cubby holes as lovers' retreats—Panama Rocks was a popular honeymooners' destination.

Also in southwestern Chautauqua County, just a few miles from the Pennsylvania border, is French Creek. Described by The Nature Conservancy as "the

Feathers of frost adorn every inch of stem on the brush along the edge of the woods at the Valentine Flats parking lot for Zoar Valley hikes. These feathers form when sufficient moisture is present on near-zero or colder nights.

most biologically diverse stream in the Northeast," the creek harbors eighty-nine species of fish and twenty-seven species of mussels. It is home to several rare species not found in other American waterways, such as spotted darter fish and northern riffleshell mussels.

The Nature Conservancy has worked closely with area farmers to protect French Creek, including helping the farmers implement riparian fences along the stream corridor to capture runoff and reduce erosion, making sure fertilizers aren't overapplied, and developing environmentally sound waste-storage structures for manure. These practices help reduce the runoff of crop nutrients, sediment, and pesticides into the water.

The Conservancy, whose motto is "saving the last great places on earth," recognizes the importance of rewarding farmers who adopt sound management practices on their farms. They have partnered with a similar but separate organization in Pennsylvania, which holds much of the creek, and with Allegheny College in Meadville, Pennsylvania, to develop strategies that benefit both the economic needs of the farmers and the environmental well-being of this ecologically significant area. With such cooperation, one is reminded of the worn but true saying, "It's amazing what can get done if nobody cares who gets the credit."

To the east, and right on the Pennsylvania border, is Allegany State Park. (It's *Allegany* State Park, but *Allegheny* National Forest next door.) As a state park, Allegany does a yeoman's job of meeting the myriad requirements of a public with wildly diverse recreational interests. A number of state parks offer a similar flexibility—trails that are used for hiking, biking, and horseback riding in summer are transformed into cross-country skiing and snowmobiling trails in winter. Helping to ensure the success of a one-size-fits-all park, and adding many more miles of unmarked trails, are the vestiges of old railroad grades, forgotten wagon roads, and former hiking trails.

Along with the Adirondack and Catskill Parks, Allegany is one of New York's three largest parks, covering about 62,000 acres. In fact, Allegany bills itself as the largest state park, but this claim probably holds up only by dint of excluding the state-owned lands that are designated as forest preserves in the Adirondack and Catskill Parks. With Allegany at virtually the opposite end of the state from the latter two, its boasts go unchallenged.

But in the end, it's the mountains and valleys (even without snazzy names) and not boasts about acreage that should get the credit in this often-overlooked corner of New York. Their beauty, ranging from grand to subtle, has inspired generations of compassionate people in both public and private life to work unselfishly for their protection.

Dense trees cloak the banks and steep walls along the Cattaraugus Creek's South Branch, viewed from The Nature Conservancy's Deer Lick Falls Preserve. A hiker makes his way upstream, carefully fording the creek and then walking the shoreline.

Facing page
At 415 feet high, the Giant Fluted Cliff in the Zoar Valley is the second tallest cliff face in western New York. The silty waters of Cattaraugus Creek flow directly under the cliff. Some of the stunted chestnut oaks on the eroded hillsides are as much as several hundred years old.

Above, left
The large boulders at the edge of this pool in the Chautauqua Gorge are out of character with the thin shale layers of the stream bed. These were probably left here when the last glaciers retreated.

Above, right
Aboveground roots struggle to hold this overhanging tree in the loose shale soils on the cliff above Valentine Flats and the Cattaraugus Creek. A fast-flowing current prevents the creek's waters from completely freezing over in the subzero February weather.

Left
The setting sun appears red in the high humidity of a hot summer's day at Long Point State Park on Chautauqua Lake.

Above, left
The roots of this tree weave in and out of the crevices of a moss-covered rock at Rock City Park, searching for nutrients.

Above, right
One of the many passageways at Rock City Park, created as the huge Olean quartz conglomerate rocks gradually slide away from one another on the softer shale layers on which they rest.

Right
This tree has managed to survive for years clinging to the rocks at Little Rock City, north of Salamanca. The rock formations are a part of the "migrating" Salamanca conglomerate.

The path at Rock City Park takes you through this opening at Three Sisters Rock. The huge rocks are spread farther apart the farther downhill they are from the main mass of quartz conglomerate.

Fallen leaves add a mosaic of autumn color to Stoddard Creek near the campground just south of Red House Lake in Allegany State Park.

Trees blown down in a storm in Allegany State Park are covered with vibrant, beautifully patterned moss.

A deer browses on the fallen fruit from an old apple tree at the edge of the forest in Allegany State Park.

Thunder Rocks, on top of one of the mountains in Allegany State Park, is part of the same cap of quartz conglomerate rock that created the "rock cities" throughout this region.

On a warm spring day at the Moss Lake Nature Sanctuary, catfish swim in the warm waters near the shore, while a Canada goose casually swims by in the background. The lake is hemmed in by a glacial moraine and contains a floating dwarf shrub bog that surrounds much of the open water.

"One can gain a wonderful feel for the real state of New York by walking across it and seeing changes from county to county in the forests, endless rises and falls, wild views up long lakes, and snippets of history left over in what is now woods or along old canals."
—Irene Szabo, President of the Finger Lakes Trail Conference, 2004

Chapter 5

THE HAND OF THE GREAT SPIRIT

THE FINGER LAKES AND A BENEDICTION

Above
A soft mist rises into the valley above Taughannock Falls on a cold winter's day. The 215-foot-high falls is the tallest of the many waterfalls in the Finger Lakes region.

Left
The Genesee River drops hundreds of feet as it passes over three gushing waterfalls in Letchworth State Park. The Middle Falls, shown here, plunges 107 feet in the central gorge.

Migratory waterfowl flock to the Montezuma National Wildlife Refuge in early spring. This pair of Canada geese is heading toward the water with their goslings in tow.

IF I WERE riding a horse and buggy a hundred years ago, my wife would have let me look around, maybe. But these days, in a car at sixty-five miles per hour or more on the New York State Thruway, she won't. So one recent April while I sat on the passenger's side, straining to glimpse the first signs of spring at warp speed, she drove west across most of New York.

The big picture, the early blush of green, was a joyous blur. But I wanted details. West of Syracuse, thickets of what I call broom grass line the highway. This five-foot-tall, plume-topped plant is really phragmites, or common reed, and if it can't be in a salt marsh, it relishes the dissolved road salt near highways. A flock of turkeys hid in a slender clearing in the reeds, and I caught a glimpse of them as we sped by. Hidden like that, they seemed right out of a Gary Larson *Far Side* cartoon, perhaps playing poker or dancing in kilts.

Long breaks in the copses of waving plumes revealed the crew-cut stubble of last year's corn fields and an occasional orchard of severely pruned fruit trees in military close-order drill. Near a farmhouse, brave daffodils stood proudly, beaten by the wind. Sheep refuse to eat them, thus keeping the daffodils safe from the stray animals.

Hawks, mostly red-tailed, were perched every few miles on poles or in tree-tops, staking out the farm fields; perhaps they were enjoying the frenetic speedway nearby. Humans—can't they go anywhere but *east and west?*

Creeks, just open, were bloated with melt-water and run-off. They parallel the highway, then duck under it. An early-bird great blue heron flying overhead seemed in search of stiller water. Seagulls, their naïve facial expressions apparent even from a short distance, were returning from wherever they had been, gliding, looking as if expecting to find mackerel and herring in the farm ponds.

Within easy view near farms were wood lots and sap buckets clinging to maple trees. A good sap run needs sunny days and cold nights, the kind of nights, come April, many of us wish would go away. But sugaring, with its work rituals, wood fires, and comradery, signals the start of spring and the end of winter.

Waves of jealousy swept over me as we bisected the Montezuma National Wildlife Refuge above Cayuga Lake, between Syracuse and Rochester. Cars parked or cruising along the roads of the refuge were filled with people who had come to this link on the Atlantic flyway. I wanted to be one of those sightseers on the other side of the fence who were taking their leisure time, unknowingly mocking us highway jitterbugs on our fool's errands.

At the refuge, migratory waterfowl, including ducks, geese, shorebirds, and a resident population of eagles, nest and rest. There are even a boat launch and public fishing sites on the New York State Barge Canal at May's Point Lock, which is within the refuge.

Today, the Montezuma National Wildlife Refuge is proof of the comebacks we can achieve as we learn more about humanity's tinkering with nature's intricate webs. For many years, however, the future looked quite dim. After the last glacial

era, ten or twelve thousand years ago, the marsh that is now the refuge approached a hundred square miles. By the early 1900s, draining and construction of a dam and the nearby Barge Canal had reduced the marsh's size to a few hundred acres.

Sometimes, unfortunately, a good economic depression and some workfare programs may be what's needed to get certain kinds of not-especially-profitable projects done. In 1937, the Bureau of Biological Survey (later the Fish and Wildlife Service) bought the 6,432 acres that now constitute the refuge, and the Civilian Conservation Corps—known as the CCs to those who worked in the Corps during the Depression—started work on water-holding dikes and other marsh restoration projects.

Decades later, at about the same time that the Environmental Protection Agency instituted a ban on the use of the pesticide DDT, the refuge played a key role in the bald-eagle restoration program in New York State. Pesticides such as DDT had had a devastating effect on the nation's eagle population. The bald eagle numbers in New York had dwindled from about seventy nesting pairs in the 1950s to just one pair by the early 1960s. In 1976, the New York State Department of Environmental Conservation, in cooperation with the U.S. Fish and Wildlife Service, began to reintroduce nesting bald eagles at Montezuma National Wildlife Refuge. Over the next four years, twenty-three bald eagles were released there. The

Fall colors glow in the last light of day at Green Lakes State Park. A solitary bench sits along the path that follows the shoreline of Green Lake, one of the park's two glacial lakes, along with neighboring Round Lake.

1,300-acre Tschache Pool serves as the eagles' home, and dozens of eaglets have taken off from a tall platform near the pool.

Today, the tranquil refuge is far removed from the days of the construction of the Barge Canal's predecessor, the Erie Canal, with its malaria and mud—and as a part-time hideout for the infamous Loomis Gang.

The Loomis Gang, consisting of ten children and their parents, was a band of horse thieves and general scoundrels who flourished from 1848 to 1866. The Loomis family evidently preferred swamps as hideouts; their home base was a 385-acre farm in a swamp near Sangerfield, not far from Utica, known as Nine Mile Swamp. A favorite tale involves one of the comely Loomis girls at a hop-pickers' dance. Other young ladies' muffs began to disappear. A daring young man lifted the Loomis girl's hoop skirts and revealed muffs on her legs from ankles to knees.

Cayuga Lake below the refuge is one of the famed Finger Lakes. The Indians who lived in the area believed that the Great Spirit laid his hand upon their country in benediction, leaving the crystal-blue Finger Lakes as his mark. Geologists, somewhat less romantically, explain these long, slender bodies of water as pre-glacial valleys whose south-flowing rivers were bottled up by glacial debris and their courses reversed.

The sides of the valleys rise abruptly to the broad back of the Allegheny Plateau. Early European settlers thought that the many rounded hillocks, sixty to a hundred feet high, were Indian burial mounds, but geologically they are drumlins, heaps of glacial debris. Tributary streams, tumbling down the steep slopes of the valleys, have cut glens and produced many waterfalls; Taughannock Falls near the head of Cayuga Lake plunges 215 feet, the highest waterfall east of the Rockies.

Near the north end of Cayuga Lake and not far from the Montezuma Refuge is Seneca Falls. For my wife and others whose passion for equal rights about equals that for nature, this historic site competes with any ordinary wildlife we might see nearby. Here Elizabeth Cady Stanton and Amelia Jenks Bloomer (who didn't invent bloomers but advocated them as a uniform for women suffragettes), along with several hundred others, met in 1848 to hold the first women's rights convention. Their cause was closely allied in the 1840s and '50s with other reform movements such as temperance and abolition. In 1850, Stanton teamed up with Susan B. Anthony, and they worked together for fifty years, laying the groundwork for women's rights.

At the opposite or south end of Cayuga Lake is Ithaca, home to Cornell University among others. The town also hosts the Cayuga Trails Club, one of numerous local hiking clubs that have adopted segments of an 880-mile foot trail stretching from Allegany State Park to the Catskills. The umbrella organization, Finger Lakes Trail Conference (FLTC), was formed in 1962 to create this trail across the state. The FLTC, which used the Appalachian Trail

A land snail works its way across a leaf at Bergen Swamp in Genesee County. The area was designated a National Natural Landmark in 1964.

Conference as its model, publishes maps and guidebooks as well as coordinating the clubs and individuals who adopt and maintain segments of the trail.

Irene Szabo, president of the FLTC, provided the following description of the Finger Lakes Trail in *Adirondac*, the magazine of the Adirondack Mountain Club, in late 2004:

> Because the trail route enjoys permissions from nearly 400 private landowners, hikers are afforded the privilege of seeing hundreds of beautiful spots normally reserved only to the owners' families, a delicious treat indeed. Mile after mile, a hiker begins to realize that many a farm or private woodlot is host to its own secret stream gully, sweet waterfall, or hilltop view. . . . Many who have been seized by the ambition to walk all the way [along the Finger Lakes Trail] started out with a little day hike an hour from home, and then just couldn't stop looking around that next curve in the path.

The Cayuga Nature Center, about six miles north of Ithaca on Route 89, overlooks Cayuga Lake and is open every day, dawn to dusk. When I was there one mid-June, the place was alive with kids—almost too alive if you wanted to see any wildlife. In the center's historic lodge, built in 1938, one sign among many pronounced, "Our counselors aren't spooky. But really rather cooky [*sic*]. I'm making lots of friends, can't wait to come again." Right under it, perhaps by way of rebuttal, is a sign that says, "You can learn many things from children—how much patience you have, for instance.—Franklin P. Adams."

Interpretation is, of course, a key part of any nature center or exhibit. One wall display tested your memory of what you'd seen if you'd toured the exhibits. For example, under "the name game," visitors were asked, "J.L., the albino rat, stands for: A) Junior lion; B) Jake's lunch; C) Jumpin' Larry."

In multiple choice tests when I don't know I always choose B, and this was correct. "J.L. was destined to be fed to a snake named Jake, but the snake never ate him! After two months he was donated to CNC." Too bad, perhaps, as the snake may have lost a dear friend. The caution on the tank holding the Burmese python read, "Please do not lean or tap on glass." This might as well have been a mandate to do just that to an adolescent boy who ran by, tapping on the fly. If caged animals ever get to rule the world, adolescent boys are in for a nasty surprise.

The center also has or is developing garden projects that include a sensory garden, an herbal and medicinal garden, and meadow gardens.

On my April high-speed trip on the Thruway, we had turned south at the westernmost Finger Lake, Conesus. Early-arriving canoeists, hard-cores, were bunched up on a boardwalk with their boats at the south end of the lake. The ice was just out; time to go paddling. And good for them—perhaps nothing looks as inscrutably purposeless as a canoe hanging in garage rafters in the depth of winter when every lake is frozen.

Above, top
The Gorge Trail meanders through Finger Lakes National Forest by idyllic settings such as this, where a white violet grows along a stream.

Above, bottom
Violets, trillium, and foamflower bloom on the forest floor in Finger Lakes National Forest, the only national forest lands in New York State.

Formed over millions of years by the Genesee River, Letchworth Gorge at Letchworth State Park is known as the "Grand Canyon of the East."

Stony Brook Glen, about fifteen miles due south of Conesus in Stony Brook State Park, is a valley, newly created since the Ice Age in the soft shale. A post-glacial stream has eroded a gorge, creating waterfalls and cliffs. The sedimentary rock pre-dates the dinosaurs and was laid in an ancient sea.

Stony Brook State Park, just 250 acres in the 1920s, has since been expanded to almost 600 acres. Much like the Montezuma National Wildlife Refuge, Stony Brook benefited from the Civilian Conservation Corps and the Works Progress Administration in the 1930s, when trails and facilities were improved.

I was struck once again by how my own birth at the end of the 1930s—a beginning for me—coincided with the end of an unfortunate economic era. Heaven knows, we don't need another economic depression of the magnitude of the thirties. But government intervention, intended primarily to provide economic support for unemployed people, resulted in unparalleled and long-lasting legacies for our natural landscape. From something bad came something good.

The prime autumn colors are brilliant in the clear sunlight at the Lower Falls of the Enfield Glen in Robert H. Treman State Park.

Above

It's easy to see why early settlers thought the 195-foot-deep Green Lake was bottomless. The two lakes in Green Lakes State Park are among only a few meromictic lakes in the United States; lakes in which the surface waters never mix with the lower layers. Dug out by glacial waterfalls, these lakes also have a three-foot-thick pink layer at about fifty-five to seventy-five feet below the surface from a combination of photosynthetic purple and green sulfur bacteria.

Left

The 167-foot falls is the best-known feature at Chittenango Falls State Park. The Chittenango ovate amber snail lives at the base of the falls—the only known location of this snail in the world. The beautiful purple loosestrife also found at the base of the falls is an invasive species that has taken over numerous wetlands in the state.

Above
The sun rising through the warm, humid summer air gives a soft glow to the marshes and fields at Montezuma National Wildlife Refuge.

Right, top
An American coot stands on an old stump amid reflections in the Main Pool at Montezuma National Wildlife Refuge.

Right, bottom
The refuge's floating reeds provide an inviting habitat for this red-winged blackbird and many other species of marsh birds.

Left
A great blue heron, searching for a snack, plucks an unsuspecting muskrat out of the marsh at the Montezuma Refuge. The heron held it for just a few seconds before the muskrat wriggled free and escaped back to the water.

Enfield Creek gently cascades over the layers of rock into the pool below Lower Falls at Robert H. Treman State Park.

Above
Sunlight filters through the trees to highlight the fallen leaves dotting the sculptured layers of rock in Watkins Glen State Park. The gorge, formed during the last Ice Age, features an array of interesting rock formations and caverns carved out by Glen Creek.

Left
The waters of Cavern Cascade drop from overhead in this view of the lower gorge at Watkins Glen State Park. A stone walkway built into the walls of the gorge takes you past some nineteen waterfalls.

Above
Letchworth Gorge was formed as glacial melt and the Genesee River cut away layers of sedimentary rock over thousands of years. Some of the cliffs in Letchworth State Park rise almost six hundred feet high.

Above, top
Whitetail deer forage in a snowy field at the edge of the woods above Middle Falls in Letchworth State Park.

Above, bottom
After a January cold spell, the Genesee River and surrounding cliffs are encased in ice at Middle Falls.

The Devil's Washtub, a glacial kettlehole pond in Mendon Ponds County Park, is surrounded by ferns and trees showing off their fall colors on a damp autumn day.

Above

Bergen Swamp, west of Rochester, is an ice-age remnant that is home to many rare and interesting plants and animals. This old cedar tree probably started life growing on a fallen log that subsequently rotted away, leaving the root and base of the tree growing in the air.

Left

Sundews, a carnivorous plant, grow on an old log along the trail in Bergen Swamp, which is managed by the Bergen Swamp Preservation Society.

> *"The land is dearer for the sea,*
> *The ocean for the shore."*
> —Lucy Larcom, *On the Beach*

Chapter 6

As the Ocean Murmurs There

Long Island, the Sound, and First Light at Montauk

Above
Phragmites growing in the moist areas behind the dunes frame the Fire Island Lighthouse in winter.

Left
The summer sun rises over the barrier dunes that border the Fire Island National Seashore along the Otis G. Pike Wilderness Area, the only federally designated wilderness area in New York State.

Rocks of many colors and compositions, as well as a few large glacial erratics, cover the beach of the David Weld Sanctuary on Long Island's North Shore.

Oɴᴇ ᴄᴏᴏʟ Aᴘʀɪʟ day, some twenty-five years ago, my friend John Roemer and I looked northward across Long Island Sound. We were waiting for the Cross Sound Ferry to take us from Orient Point, at the northeastern tip of the Island, across to New London, Connecticut. We could see the Orient Point Lighthouse nearby, five degrees out of kilter.

We were oblivious to the fact that we were also close to Orient Beach State Park and a rare maritime forest with black-jack oak trees, red cedar, and prickly pear cactus, now a protected species.

Cactus? On Long Island, in New York? The significance was wasted on us. All we could think about, standing with our bicycles at the ferry slip, was four or five meals a day and getting to Boston to run the Boston Marathon. Ah—youth!

But this was our first glimpse and smell of big water, salt water. In our last few days, even at cycling pace, we had seen so many changes of scenery and environment that sorting everything out was nearly impossible. We were riding a route that started in Maryland and took us through New York City. Before we started, we were terrified that New York City traffic would be our Waterloo. We would be hit by cars, robbed, left crippled and broke.

Fortunately, for us at least, that year the city was hit by a transit strike. The busses were gone, and one lane of downtown streets was reserved for bicycles. Now we were just part of a human-powered wave of bikes thumbing its figurative nose at bus stink and behemoth amounts of automotive traffic. Bicycles were everywhere, from kids' banana-seated bikes with small wheels, ridden by leather-jacketed artist types toting huge portfolio cases, to full-bore racing bikes, cutting and dicing through traffic like messenger-delivery cyclists. Yes—humanity in the ascendancy! *Vive le strike!*

We shot through Manhattan, cops waving us through red lights, ecstatic at our good fortune, and spent the night somewhere on the way to Long Island in the only motel we could find. In the next two days, riding many times over and under the Long Island Expressway, we hop-scotched to our jumping-off point for New England, Orient Point.

There our noses told us we were in a new and different environment from the farms of Maryland or even eastern Long Island's then still common duck farms, with their soupçon of salt air mixed with *odeur du canard*.

Stretching some 125 miles from the Verrazano Narrows Bridge in Brooklyn to Montauk Point, but only 20 miles across at its widest, Long Island contains an almost-bewildering array of scenery and habitats. Beyond the droves of city folk who head out to the posh Hamptons on summer weekends, the island is a year-round home to myriad bird species, aquatic animals, and diverse vegetation.

If you squint and look at a map of Long Island, you might see an alligator (gentler squinters see a whale) facing right with its mouth open. The long under-jaw—the South Shore—goes to Montauk Point, and the eastern tip of the upper one ends at Orient Point. Each alligator jaw ends in a state park.

Over the years, Long Island has seen many groups and individuals working everywhere on the figurative alligator to preserve the island's wildlife and habitats. In 1987, Long Island Sound between New York and Connecticut was designated an "Estuary of National Significance" under a clause of the federal Clean Water Act that protects significant estuaries from pollution, development, and overuse. (An estuary is a partially enclosed body of water where freshwater rivers and streams flow into ocean salt water. Other well-known estuaries include Tampa Bay, Chesapeake Bay, and Puget Sound.)

The Atlantic Ocean and adjacent Long Island Sound are huge and must be revered for what they are in their entirety. But when it comes to land-based efforts to protect our environment, I hold the notion, right or wrong, that small, intimate "vest-pocket" parks and preserves are loved by their often few visitors even more, per capita, than the big ones. If that's true, maybe it's because urban noise and the source of whatever else drifts or forces its way in are often not far away from these small, spiritual oases; the contrast with what is around them is even more pronounced. I've often wondered how these beloved places came to be, especially in New York City and on Long Island.

Looking at the history of some of the preserves on Long Island, I saw an interesting pattern: Lands that had been privately owned estates or hunting clubs

A male fiddler crab waves his large claw in a courtship ritual, hoping to gain the attention of a female fiddler. This colony of fiddler crabs resides at Mashomack Preserve on Shelter Island.

often were later converted to nature preserves for all to enjoy. One notable example, on the North Shore of the island, just above where our alligator's tail might start, is Oyster Bay National Wildlife Refuge. The refuge surrounds Sagamor Hill National Historic Site, which from 1885 to 1919 was the home of Theodore Roosevelt, founder of the National Wildlife Refuge System. New York's only remaining commercial oyster farm operates on the refuge, producing 90 percent of the state's oysters. Sea turtles and harbor seals can also be seen at the refuge, and Oyster Bay is a popular winter habitat and migratory stop for waterfowl and other birds.

Almost perfectly due south of Oyster Bay, or about where our alligator's hind leg would join, Tackapausha Preserve at Seaford was Nassau County's first nature preserve. It was initiated in 1938 by George Peters, the Deputy Commissioner of Public Works, with less than sixty acres. Peters's intentions were quite practical: to preserve a portion of the Seaford Creek watershed and prevent roads and homes in the area from flooding during periods of high water. The commissioner understood that good conservation equaled fewer headaches. Through the years, more acres were added, in ever-smaller increments—almost thirty in 1955, almost six in 1962, less than two-thirds of an acre in 1966, and one-third of an acre in 1992. Nevertheless, every addition should be viewed as an accomplishment.

Tackapausha Preserve is located on glacial outwash plain, a mostly flat terrain composed of sand and gravel deposited by runoff from the glacier that stopped just north of the park; today it holds the largest remaining stand of Atlantic white cedar in Nassau County. Human history on the preserve, much of it recent, has presented many challenges, challenges that have been met with care and creativity. In the 1970s, for example, forest areas were cleared to make storage space for construction equipment being used during the installation of sewer lines. The scenario seems almost "Fellini-esque," but when the project was done, the site was replanted with native tallgrass prairie grasses and wildflowers. This area, part of the Hempstead Plains,

The colors of fall are perfectly mirrored in a small pond of outflow waters in Connetquot River State Park Preserve.

is the only naturally occurring prairie east of the Allegheny Mountains, prairie that once covered sixty thousand acres of Nassau County. Our hats are off to George Peters.

Long Island's largest state park, Connetquot River State Park Preserve, is about twenty-five miles east of Tackapausha, near Oakdale (where our mythical alligator would drag its belly), extending over more than 3,400 acres. The history of this park suggests a more leisurely time, actual or not. Members of the South Side Sportsmen's Club used the former Snedecor's Tavern, built there in 1820, as a clubhouse from 1860 to 1973. The Oakdale Gristmill dates back to 1760; it ran for a century, milling corn and wheat and sawing lumber, the first essential tasks in most early communities.

Today the remaining buildings sport chipping sparrows on the lawn and barn swallows undulating across the mowed fields. Long Island is relatively narrow here, and from the park you can get on the Greenbelt Trail, a thirty-four-mile north-south trail that goes from the Governor Alfred E. Smith Sunken Meadow State Park on the North Shore to Heckscher State Park in the south near East Islip.

Continuing east on the South Shore, the salt marshes of the Wertheim National Wildlife Refuge, combined with adjacent state-owned salt marsh, form the largest continuous salt marsh on Long Island. The other half of this salt marsh, near

The Dwarf Pine Barrens of Long Island are one of only three such ecosystems in the world. Pitch pine, scrub oak, pine barrens heather, and scattered blueberry bushes are a few of the plants that manage to survive in the very porous, sandy soil.

Shirley, is in the central core of Long Island's Pine Barrens. Pitch pine is the dominant tree species, with oak-pine (a seeming oxymoron, like the hawk-owl of the far north) and white, red, and black oaks among the upland shrub and grasslands.

Cecile and Maurice Wertheim used the area that is now the biggest part of the refuge as a private reserve for waterfowl hunting. They donated their 2,550 acres in 1947. More donated land, the Wellington Tract, was added in 1974; 129 additional acres, the South Haven property, in 1998; followed by another 19 acres in 1999. One of the last remaining duck farms on Long Island is part of the refuge.

The twenty-two-acre Sayville National Wildlife Refuge, a division of Wertheim, is located on land suitable for the endangered plant sandplain gerardia. This refuge was a federal land transfer in 1993 from, quixotically, the Federal Aviation Administration.

As we reach the head of our metaphorical alligator, we encounter several innovative organizations working to protect Long Island's ecology. The Riverhead Foundation for Marine Research and Preservation (near the alligator's eye) has as its

The Nature Conservancy's Daniel R. Davis Sanctuary is part of Long Island's rare Central Pine Barrens. Pitch pine often has tufts of needles growing directly from its trunk, almost as if decorated for Christmas.

primary mission the rescue, rehabilitation, and release of sick and injured sea turtles, seals, dolphins, and whales. Their Stranding Program cares for over 150 animals a year; most are returned to the ocean. Pulling out all the stops to achieve their mission, the Riverhead Foundation offers an adoption program for animals in the Stranding Program, whereby donors receive photographs of the adopted animal, a biography, and a certificate.

Another example of Long Island's legacy of private lands converted to nature preserves for all to enjoy, Conscience Point National Wildlife Refuge was established in 1971 as a gift from Stanley Howard. It's located on the north shore of Long Island's south fork, about where my alligator would have a molar. The grasslands on Conscience Point's sixty acres are a habitat model for maritime grasslands, habitat which is disappearing on Long Island. Maritime grasslands are native and include switch grass, little bluestem grass, poverty grass, hairgrass, and the still-anomalous-to-my-eye prickly pear cactus. The grasslands are being managed specifically to attract grassland-dependent birds such as grasshopper and savannah sparrows, eastern meadowlark, and bobolink.

The Elizabeth A. Morton National Wildlife Refuge was established from a 187-acre gift from the Morton family in 1954. Most of the refuge is located on a peninsula surrounded by Noyack and Little Peconic Bays (dangerously placed in its mouth, were my alligator to chomp down) and serves as an important corridor for a variety of migratory birds. The waters around the refuge also provide a critical habitat for young Kemp's Ridley sea turtles and even occasional huge loggerhead sea turtles.

The process of accretion of all these lands might be, on one hand, a dry narrative of deed transfers and lawyer's bills, but on the other, an exhilarating story of visionary individuals seeing a chance to preserve rapidly disappearing land and

The sand and clay of the bluffs at Montauk Point are continually being eroded away by the waves of the Atlantic Ocean, while the rocks and boulders remain as monuments to the forces of the glaciers.

habitat—essentially heeding Aldo Leopold's advice that as we dismember our planet willy-nilly to not throw away any of the pieces. Indeed, these generous visionaries have worked to reassemble lands that, in most cases, belong together.

I've experienced our Atlantic coast from Maine to Florida. Recently, I sat back and tried to decide what among the vast and contemplation-inducing coastal beaches, bays, and ocean was the single most personally memorable feature of all. The abject answer: sand fleas. I still vividly remember camping in the open on the dunes of Ocean City, Maryland, one early March. Getting the jump on the tourist season gave me the choice of the winter's flotsam and jetsam. Manmade treasures from distant lands and strange natural treasures from the ocean's depths were mine to pick from as they floated to the shore.

But the sand fleas had their pick of me. The sand flea—beach flea, hop-a-long—is a crustacean, not an insect, less than an eighth of an inch long, and can jump up to twenty inches. Their tiny size puts them up there with the Adirondacks' blackflies and no-see-ums in annoyance-to-size ratio. The fleas are abundant in decaying seaweed that washes up to the high-tide mark, right about where I camped that March. They hit their stride in the evening and at night—just when someone in the open on the beach is trying to sleep. Sand fleas range up and down the Atlantic coast, and I've made their pesky acquaintance everywhere I've gone. Nature's most instructive lessons are sometimes small ones, from small creatures.

Probably any fisherman or beachcomber could have told me about sand fleas and how to avoid them. Instead, they might say forget the fleas, look at the early morning sun, an orange orb on the eastern horizon blazing the start of a new day. Or sit just offshore in a small boat, swaying gently, far from sand fleas and terrestrial cares.

That, they might say, is one good way to enjoy this part of New York.

Above
Pitch pine, oaks, and underbrush are covered with a mantle of fresh snow along the boardwalk near the Fire Island Lighthouse.

Left
Wind-blown grasses form patterns in the sand at Heckscher State Park on Great South Bay. The park is the start of the Long Island Greenbelt Trail, which extends north across the island to Sunken Meadow State Park.

Facing page
The first light of morning highlights the shoreline grasses near the outlet of the Nissequogue River at Kings Point, at the northeast corner of Governor Alfred E. Smith Sunken Meadow State Park.

The deck at the Fire Island Wilderness Visitor Center at Smith Point offers a panoramic view of Fire Island. The Atlantic Ocean is on the left, and the Great South Bay is on the right. This area is home to the endangered piping plover and a diverse wildlife population.

A rainbow gracefully arches above Bass Creek near where it empties into Shelter Island Sound on The Nature Conservancy's Mashomack Preserve.

Above
Young swans charge up a flow on the Connet-quot River near the trout hatchery at the state park preserve.

Left
While fall leaves drift downstream on the sur-face of the water, the trout below the hatchery at Connetquot River State Park Preserve swim back and forth looking for food washing downstream.

Above

An osprey soars in front of the rising sun to greet its mate on the nesting pole at Merrill Lake Sanctuary. This Nature Conservancy preserve is the premier birdwatcher's location in the East Hampton area.

Right

A great egret fishes along the rocky shoreline of Nicolls Point at Mashomack Preserve. The preserve's ten miles of coastline are home to myriad bird species, including osprey, eagles, least terns, and the endangered piping plover.

Above
High cirrus clouds, warning of an approaching storm, stretch across the sky above the "Walking Dunes" at Hither Hills State Park. These dunes, at Napeague Bay in Block Island Sound, are constantly shifting in the wild ocean winds, gradually covering over the old oak forests here. It is believed that the cutting of trees along the shore by early settlers allowed the dunes to build up.

Left
Goldenrod blooms among the heather on an early fall day at the Hither Hills Walking Dunes. A low section of the dunes includes a freshwater marsh with cranberries growing among the reeds.

Low tide at Montauk State Park exposes snails as well as kelp and other seaweeds that cover the boulders at the water's edge.

Above, top
Harbor seals, ringed seals, and harp seals bask together in the warm sun on an offshore rock near Montauk Point.

Above, bottom
Just after the sun peered above the eastern horizon, a seal flopped up onto the exposed rock to catch a few rays and enjoy the golden warmth of the rising sun.

"The winds', the birds', the ocean-floods',
The City's voice itself is soft like Solitude's."
—Percy Bysshe Shelley, from *Stanzas Written in Dejection Near Naples,* 1818

Chapter 7

HIDDEN OASES AMONG BRICK AND GLASS

NEW YORK CITY, FOREVER WILD

Above
Mating horseshoe crabs find an ideal habitat in the sandy grasses along the Jamaica Bay shoreline. I cut a number of them free from partially buried fishing nets they had become ensnared in.

Left
With the city skyline in the distance, Canada geese feed in the grasses at Jamaica Bay National Wildlife Refuge.

I N ADDITION TO our policy, you have a constituency." Ah, one little word that speaks volumes—*constituency*. Adrian Benepe, Commissioner of the New York City Department of Parks and Recreation, had just identified his ace in the hole. The City—residents here usually say they live in "New York" or the "City," meaning New York City, dismissing the inconsequential hinterlands—has forty-eight protected preserves, totaling more than 8,700 acres, and in 2000, these preserves were designated "Forever Wild" by Benepe's department. Forever Wild is the same phrase long applied to state lands in the upstate Adirondack and Catskill Parks, a protection guaranteed by the state constitution. Such a designation would seem to assure protection to the City's preserves in perpetuity.

But while the words are the same, in New York City Forever Wild is a policy with, unfortunately, no legal force. "A future administration could undo it," Benepe admitted to the *New York Times* in 2004. That's where the clout of a constituency comes in, and what Benepe is counting on. In other words, the force and will of people who value the preserves, some very small, scattered among New York City's five boroughs, will ensure that they remain forever wild.

Officially protected only as parkland, the status of the preserves allows for, among other uses, ball fields and playgrounds. Even when used in this relatively benign manner, however, nature has a way of reclaiming her own, back-to-wild status. In Queens' Forest Park, for example, a swamp in a park hollow was converted into a baseball field, but regular flooding returned it to its earlier existence as a woodland kettle pond (a glacial legacy), sporting floating-hearts with their water-lily-like leaves and five-petaled flowers.

In Brooklyn, an even more radical reversal took place. A great deal of 798-acre Marine Park—mostly saltwater wetland—was once landfill. Today grasses dominate the vegetation, including graceful phragmites with their broom-like plumes. This invasive grass, also called common reed, had long been considered as undesirable as a landfill in a natural area.

But after a second look, naturalists found that the plant indeed has value: Phragmites purifies the air and soil it occupies, provides cover for animals (as I saw with turkeys on my way to the Finger Lakes), and drops seeds that sustain wildlife. True, wildlife will probably eat whatever else is available first—but surely phragmites beats a landfill.

The best-known park among the City's forty-eight is, of course, Central Park in Manhattan. Even here, in a park created by Frederick Law Olmsted and Calvert Vaux, and called a "glorious fake" made from shantytowns and swampland, nature has returned to restake her claim. The name of a stream in the park, the Loch, gives a hint of the metamorphosis: Loch is a Scottish word for lake. Olmsted and Vaux indeed intended, and at first created, a long narrow lake. But over the past century, the lake reverted to a stream. Running through the Ravine, the only stream valley in Central Park, the Loch is flanked by a deciduous forest of oak, hickory, maple, and

ash. Stunning, glossy ibis can be seen on the thickets of accumulated silt on islands in the stream.

Olmsted and Vaux also designed Prospect Park Preserve in Brooklyn. In their design for this 208-acre park, they combined two areas of existing forest and a network of wetlands. The wetlands are a combination of park design and ice age glacial terrain. Initially the park designers planted many evergreens in an attempt to create an Adirondack landscape, but the evergreens didn't flourish. In their place now are native oaks, such as pin oak, and non-native Norway maples and sycamore maples.

Manhattan's Inwood Hill Park, including Shorakapok Preserve, contains some of the few remaining acres of natural forest and salt marsh left on the island. Salt marshes once surrounded the island that came to be Manhattan. This 136-acre park, located at the island's northern end, holds some of the largest tulip trees in the city. A moist valley between two rock ridges comes alive with wildflowers in spring before the forest canopy leafs out overhead. Downy yellow violet, bloodroot, and Dutchman's breeches bloom, and many of over 150 species of birds seen here begin their return.

Urban forests have their unique problems. The high proportion of nearby paved surfaces can lead to flash flooding, the speed of the runaway water accelerating soil erosion. To combat these challenges, the Parks Department has a Natural

This idyllic wilderness path can be found right in the heart of Manhattan. Central Park's Ravine offers a series of pathways through a part of the park that has been designated Forever Wild.

The New Jersey Palisades are a majestic sight across the Hudson River from the Shorakapok Preserve in Inwood Hill Park. Inwood Hill is one of New York State's bald eagle reintroduction sites.

Resources Group, including a SWAT-like forest restoration team dispatched to the city's parks; Inwood Hill serves as the base for the operation.

The City's largest park property, three times the size of Central Park, is Pelham Bay Park. This park includes thirteen miles of saltwater shoreline along Long Island Sound. Located in the Bronx, Pelham Bay Park Preserves links the Thomas Pell Wildlife Refuge and Hunter Island Marine Sanctuary. Nearly two hundred acres of salt marsh benefit humans by acting as natural filtration systems, absorbing fertilizers and reducing erosion.

The existence and protection of the Hunter Island Marine Sanctuary owes much to Commissioner Benepe's notion of constituency. In 1963 the City began landfill operations near here on Tallapoosa Point in Pelham Bay Park. Plans were made in 1966 to expand the landfill even further, which would have made it the second biggest refuse disposal site next to Fresh Kills in Staten Island. Bronx Councilmember Mario Merola led widespread community opposition to the plan, resulting in creation of the park's sanctuaries by a local law signed by Mayor John Lindsay in 1967.

The task of creating and keeping preserves in New York City must be accomplished in the face of even greater pressures than are confronted in many other places. The immense refuse-disposal needs of the City, and the small number of sites available, highlight the miracles of constituency and protection in an instance such as the Hunter Island Marine Sanctuary. Such miracles call for eternal vigilance and organized political action. Frankly, living in the six-million acre Adirondack Park, I have only the barest inkling of the energy and organization that have gone into the creation and protection of the City's preserves.

But Central Park has long been close to my heart. For twenty-five years, at least once a year, I had to go to New York City on business. For this rural rube, the city was a percussive jolt. In the mornings I would jog in Central Park, unable to make eye contact with anybody, and look and listen for some of the over two hundred species of birds that have been seen there. The Essex Hotel sign on Central Park South and a statue of a mounted horseman were my landmarks back to my hotel. I couldn't imagine how the people kept up their frenetic action day in and day out. Surely, the whole tableau was an elaborate play, staged for my benefit, collapsing in a heap on my departure.

Getting from place to place during my work day in Manhattan, I adopted my persona of Feral Man. In ordinary dress and behavior, I fit in. But unknown to everybody around me, I was living years before—*many* years before. I was keeping company with walruses, giant bison, and huge ground sloths and mastadons, all sashaying contentedly along with me. Tapirs, musk oxen, and peccaries—my menagerie and I, time-warped tourists, peered in windows on Fifth Avenue and waited for traffic lights to change. Somehow we went unnoticed.

These animals—all of them—lived in the City or nearby, some as recently as twenty-five thousand years ago. By the time Peter Minuit bought Manhattan Island from the Indians for trinkets in 1626, all these creatures were long gone.

While flying out of the City at night, up and away over miles of lights and streams of creeping cars, I got a real idea of the City's population. I knew that scattered below, near the surging, pulsing waves of humanity, were preserves such as Central Park, part of the primeval ground my menagerie and I once roamed.

Looking below from the plane each time I left the City, I said goodbye for now to my antediluvian friends. Feral Man gave a little wave, a wave none of my fellow passengers ever noticed.

At dawn, a flock of Canada geese fly over the West Pond area in the Jamaica Bay National Wildlife Refuge. Located within the Gateway National Recreation Area, it is the only refuge managed by the National Park Service.

Pelham Bay Park marks the southernmost coastal outcropping of Hartland schist, giving the Hunter Island shoreline features reminiscent of the rocky New England coastline, with tidal pools, rocky bays, and glacial erratics. The Hartland schist is the exposed bedrock that formed here some five hundred million years ago.

Shorakapok Preserve in northern Manhattan contains some of the only natural forest left on the island. This tulip poplar near the top of Inwood Hill is one of the many giant trees that grow here. Some trees in the preserve tower more than one hundred feet tall, with trunks as much as six feet in diameter.

Above, top
Two painted turtles and a mallard duck enjoy a sunny spring day at Prospect Park in Brooklyn.

Above, bottom
A fallen oak leaf transforms the exposed marbled schist into a work of art at Pelham Bay Park in the Bronx.

Above, top
Asters are in full bloom in a wildflower garden bordering the southern edge of the Central Park Ravine in Manhattan.

Above, bottom
Vibrant autumn reds illuminate the oaks at Lemon Creek Preserve in the 2,800-acre Greenbelt of Staten Island.

Sweet gum, oak, phragmites, and bulrushes line the shore of Little Alley Pond in Alley Pond Park in Queens. More than three hundred species of birds and other wildlife are present in this preserve, which includes both freshwater and saltwater habitats.

Sweet gum is a fast-growing southern tree species found in some of New York City's parks. This pair is reaching for the sky in Alley Pond Park in Queens.

A majestic old willow—another tree species commonly associated with southern climes—arches gracefully over the freshwater pond near the Alley Pond Environmental Center.

A blue heron fishes along exposed mud flats at low tide in the lagoon at the Hunter Island Marine Sanctuary in Pelham Bay Park.

Chapter 8

NEW YORK:
THE SPIRIT
AND THE BEAUTY

Above
The shoreline dunes of the Fire Island National Seashore offer protection from the ocean's fury during Atlantic storms.

Left
Bear Mountain provides a spectacular natural setting within a short drive of New York City. Bear Mountain State Park was the result of an organized community effort to preserve this beautiful stretch of the Hudson Highlands.

Alpine stewards have been placing small rocks around alpine vegetation on Algonquin Peak and elsewhere in the Adirondacks to help the summits recover from the erosion caused by hikers tramping over the vegetation.

I LEAD A charmed life in a charmed place. I have to try to remember that, to tell myself that every day. Some days I forget. But something outside the window, say, happens to remind me where I am. The start and finish of a winter day is a perfect example—at dusk, the alpenglow on MacKenzie Mountain out the window over the kitchen sink brings me up short.

What are the right words for colors I can't name, or that have no precise names? I see the reddish-pink-orange of the setting sun, colors bounced at an oblique angle off the crystals in the snow, colors muted by the grays of encroaching dusk. In the new dawn, I see the same colors—almost—out a different window. All right, the color is alpenglow, that's its name—a color and a name so precious we use it only for this singular, majestic sight.

At odds with such ineffable beauty is a sort of sad conversation I have with young people here at home. They say they have to get out of this "hick town" and go somewhere—anywhere—where the action is. They are right—they do, because they believe they do. At least for now. Many come back in a few years if there is any chance of a decent job, sometimes even if there isn't. I will never say I told you so; they had to see for themselves.

Because here, we call the rest of the world the "Outside World," the world over the "Blue Line," that park boundary that exists only on maps. We make jokes; we say we see bleariness and confusion in the eyes of people who have been "outside," if only for half a day: "Aha, been outside the Blue Line, haven't you?" We call the Outside World a scary place; we are only half kidding.

Why? One answer is subtle, almost a riff on the old joke about the lighthouse keeper who awakened from a sound sleep one night when his fog horn missed a single blast, and shouted, "What was that?" Drive into the Adirondack Park from any direction and you will notice—maybe not right away, as it's subtle—there are no billboards. None. And if you see a neon sign along the highway—and you can drive for miles without seeing one—you can bet that sign was already there about thirty years ago, grandfathered in when the new laws on signs went into effect.

Things such as these are part of my charmed life. They are never so apparent to me as when I leave the Adirondacks to go see the Outside World. Away from home, I get paranoid and fear that my townspeople will somehow find me out for what I am—whatever I am that is so awful—and not let me come back. I race home, safe, and hide out back in my little log cabin.

Here in the Adirondacks, one of our biggest environmental threats, acid precipitation, comes not from regional sources but the Midwest. Their tall industrial stacks, many coal burning, emit nitrogen oxides and sulphur dioxide, shooting them up into the prevailing westerlies. Carried eastward, the pol-

lution falls with rain or snow (or sleet or fog or cloud vapor) onto our mountains and lakes. Acidification of soil and bedrock causes heavy metals such as mercury and aluminum to become soluble and end up in our water. We are told our fish are unfit to eat. The magnitude of the problem seems beyond our ability to deal with it.

I read of the ongoing battle here to preserve what we have, the push-pull between preservation and development. If there were ever a place where preservation and wildness and wilderness equals economic benefit, this is it. But our mix of private and public lands with no apparent rhyme or reason causes endless management headaches. We could have had rhyme and reason *if only* a couple of hundred years ago they had had enough sense to buy up all the land and create the Park *then*. Right—and if turtles had wings they wouldn't bump their bums as they drag from place to place.

Coming at us on our blind side is the electronic age, where our intellect—driven by some imperative gone wrong, rational but no longer sane—outstrips our biology. Virtual reality, as close as our keyboard, is preferred over real life. Warm and dry, we pull up scenes of cold and wet places, pictures with bugs and mud, and sweaty or cold people. We don't have to go there in person—there it is on the screen.

The maze of contoured rock in the upper gorge at Watkins Glen State Park inspires wonder in nature lovers of all ages.

So, should we despair? Of course not. Even in the Outside World, I see people hunkered down where they feel they belong, people laboring to preserve and cherish that piece of the world, however small, they have adopted in their hearts. They feel a tie to the land, part of the same impulse that seizes us in early spring when we scratch in the dirt, planting flowers and vegetables, an uncontrollable energy driving us toward life and creation that results in very sore winter-atrophied muscles the day after.

Despair? Margaret Mead said, "Never doubt that a small group of thoughtful, committed citizens can change the world. Indeed, it's the only thing that ever has." Are we—you and I—in that group?

Despair? Not as long as some of us prefer bugs and mud and sweat and cold over a second-rate imitation on a computer screen. Not as long as there are vest-pocket parks with just a bench or two. Not as long as there are preserves that don't even have a bench, parks hardly anybody knows are there, flowers blooming year after year, rarely seen.

While some may choose to steer clear of the area's commercialization and colorful light displays—viewed here from the Goat Island observation area of Niagara Falls State Park—the year-round natural beauty of Niagara Falls has been celebrated for centuries.

Despair? Not as long as there were once people who planted lilacs where nothing now remains but cellar holes, people with houses and children and often hardscrabble lives, people gone and mostly nameless to us now. Not as long as there are people such as my friend Carl Heilman, who captures the natural beauty of

our state in stunning photographs, such as those in this book. During his odyssey, Carl drove almost fifteen thousand miles to dozens of natural and inspiring places around the state. A New York State resident for years, he said, humbled, "I'll never look at New York the same way again." I told him how I had kissed the ground at the New York State border after three thousand miles of cycling. He just smiled, understanding completely. For us, now the whole state is our home.

Despair? My New York tally of places and people, and ideas and actions, and creatures and vistas, and vision and hope, has no end. Such a list ranges from my grudgingly respected sand fleas on the coasts, to the summit of Mount Marcy, to the shores of Lake Erie. The sounds alone—geese calling on their way south in October, and again on their return in the spring; the thunderous booms of the water beneath the ice in January; the loon's cry—a whole orchestral score could be made up of New York's sounds. I close my eyes and hear those sounds.

Her sights know no bounds: the sight of alpenglow, or seeing the beauty of a lone rose in a weed thicket, or the wavelets veering out from a canoe's bow, or the endless horizon of a Great Lake.

These cherished places, their sights, sounds, and smells—this beautiful, heavenly land. "Behold, from henceforth all generations shall call me blessed."

Despair? Impossible—not an option. Seized by awe, tears in our eyes, humbled by the beauty and opportunities everywhere around us, we dismiss despair out of hand, exalting in celebration and wonder. Indeed—behold!

West Pond in the Jamaica Bay National Wildlife Refuge overlooks the Brooklyn and Manhattan skyline in the distance—a reminder of the delicate intersection of the worlds of nature and human civilization.

CONSERVATION RESOURCES AND NATURE ORGANIZATIONS

Adirondack Mountain Club
301 Hamilton Street
Albany, NY 12210
(518) 449-3870
www.adk.org

Adirondack Council
103 Hand Avenue, Suite 3
Elizabethtown, NY 12932
(877) 873-2240
www.adirondackcouncil.org

Appalachian Mountain Club
New York–North Jersey
Chapter
5 Tudor City Place
New York, NY 10017
(212) 986-1430
www.amc-ny.org

Association for the
Protection of the
Adirondacks
897 St. Davids Lane
Niskayuna, NY 12309
(518) 377-1452
www.protectadks.org

Audubon New York
200 Trillium Lane
Albany, NY 12203
(518) 869-9731
ny.audubon.org

Catskill Mountain Club
P.O. Box 558
Pine Hill, NY 12465
www.catskillmountainclub
.org

Catskill Watershed
Corporation
905 Main Street
Margaretville, NY 12455
(877) 928-7433
or (845) 586-1400
www.cwconline.org

The Central Park
Conservancy
14 East 60th Street
New York, NY 10022
(212) 310-6600
www.centralparknyc.org

Citizens Environmental
Coalition
33 Central Avenue
Albany, NY 12210
(518) 462-5527
cectoxic.home.igc.org

Environmental Advocates of
New York
353 Hamilton Street
Albany, NY 12210
(800) SAVE-NYS or
(518) 462-5526
www.eany.org

Finger Lakes Land Trust
202 East Court Street
Ithaca, NY 14850
(607) 275-9487
www.fllt.org

Finger Lakes Trail
Conference
6111 Visitor Center Road
Mt. Morris, NY 14510
(585) 658-9320
www.fingerlakestrail.org

Great Lakes United
Buffalo State College,
Cassety Hall
1300 Elmwood Avenue
Buffalo, NY 14222
(716) 886-0142
www.glu.org

Greenbelt Conservancy
200 Nevada Avenue
Staten Island, NY 10306
(718) 667-2165
www.sigreenbelt.org

Group for the South Fork
2442 Main Street
P.O. Box 569
Bridgehampton, NY 11932
(631) 537-1400
www.thehamptons.com/
group

Hudson River Sloop
Clearwater, Inc.
112 Little Market Street
Poughkeepsie, NY 12601
(845) 454-7673
www.clearwater.org

Land Trust Alliance
Northeast Program Field
Office
110 Spring Street
Saratoga Springs, NY 12866
(518) 587-0774
www.lta.org

Long Island Pine
Barrens Society
P.O. Box 429
Manorville, NY 11949
(631) 369-3300
www.pinebarrens.org

Natural Resources Defense
Council
40 West 20th Street
New York, NY 10011
(212) 727-2700
www.nrdc.org

The Nature Conservancy
New York State Office
570 Seventh Avenue
Suite 601
New York, NY 10018
(212) 381-2190
www.nature.org/newyork

New York–New Jersey Trail
Conference
156 Ramapo Valley Road,
Route 202
Mahwah, NJ 07430
(201) 512-9348
www.nynjtc.org

New York Rivers United
P.O. Box 1460
Rome, NY 13442
(315) 339-2097
www.newyorkriversunited
.org

New Yorkers for Parks
457 Madison Avenue
New York, NY 10022
(212) 838-9410
www.ny4p.org

Open Space Institute
1350 Broadway, Suite 201
New York, NY 10018
(212) 629-3981
www.osiny.org

Parks and Trails New York
29 Elk Street
Albany, NY 12207
(518) 434-1583
www.ptny.org

Peconic Land Trust
296 Hampton Road
P.O. Box 1776
Southampton, NY 11969
(631) 283-3195
www.peconiclandtrust.org

Residents' Committee to
Protect the Adirondacks
P.O. Box 27
North Creek, NY 12853
(518) 251-4257
www.rcpa.org

Riverkeeper
P.O. Box 130
Garrison, NY 10524
(800) 21-RIVER
www.riverkeeper.org

Scenic Hudson, Inc.
One Civic Center Plaza,
Suite 200
Poughkeepsie, NY 12601
(845) 473-4440
www.scenichudson.org

Sierra Club, Atlantic Chapter
353 Hamilton Street
Albany, NY 12210
(518) 426-9144
www.newyork.sierraclub.org

Tug Hill Commission
Dulles State Office Building
317 Washington Street
Watertown, NY 13601
(315) 785-2380/2570
www.tughill.org

The Urban Rangers
New York City Department
of Parks and Recreation
The Arsenal
Central Park
830 5th Avenue
New York, NY 10021
www.nycgovparks.org

The Wildlife Conservation
Society
2300 Southern Boulevard
Bronx, NY 10460
(718) 220-5100
www.wcs.org

Hundred Acre Pond shore-
line, Mendon Ponds Park,
south of Rochester.

BIBLIOGRAPHY

Anderson, Scott Edward. *Walks in Nature's Empire: Exploring the Nature Conservancy's Preserves in New York State.* Woodstock, Vt.: The Countryman Press, 1995.

Beebe, William. *Unseen Life of New York As A Naturalist Sees It.* New York: Duell, Sloan and Pearce, 1953.

Burdick, Neal S., series ed. *Guide to Adirondack Trails.* 8 vols. Lake George, N.Y.: Adirondack Mountain Club, 1992–1994.

Ehling, William P. *50 Hikes in Central New York.* Woodstock, Vt.: Backcountry Guides, 1995.

Ehling, William P. *50 Hikes in Western New York.* Woodstock, Vt.: Backcountry Guides, 1990.

Experience the Wonders of Nature: A Visitor's Guide to Long Island's Last Great Places. N.P.: The Nature Conservancy, 2000.

Gallagher, Winifred. *The Power of Place: How Our Surroundings Shape Our Thoughts, Emotions, and Actions.* New York: HarperPerennial, 1994.

Green, Stella, and H. Neil Zimmerman. *50 Hikes in the Lower Hudson Valley.* Woodstock, Vt.: Backcountry Guides, 2002.

Harmon, Chris, Matt Levy, and Gabrielle Antoniadis. *Preserve Guide, Eastern New York Chapter: Lower Hudson Region.* N.P.: The Nature Conservancy, 2000.

Kershner, Bruce. *Secret Places: Scenic Treasures of Western New York and Southern Ontario.* Dubuque, Iowa: Kendall/Hunt Publishing, 1994.

Knight, Frank. *New York Wildlife Viewing Guide.* Helena, Mont.: Falcon Publishing, 1998.

Leopold, Aldo. *A Sand County Almanac.* New York: Oxford University Press, 1987.

McAllister, Lee. *Hiking Long Island.* Mahwah, N.J.: New York–New Jersey Trail Conference, 2001.

Merrill, Arch. *The Ridge.* Rochester, N.Y.: The Democrat and Chronicle, 1944.

New York: A Guide to the Empire State. New York: Oxford University Press, 1940.

New York Atlas and Gazetteer. 6th ed. Freeport, Maine: Delorme Mapping Co., 2001.

New York Walk Book. Mahwah, N.J.: New York–New Jersey Trail Conference, 2001.

Sanders, Scott Russell. *Staying Put: Making a Home in a Restless World.* Boston: Beacon Press, 1993.

Sauer, Peter, ed. *Finding Home: Writing on Nature and Culture From Orion Magazine.* Boston: Beacon Press, 1992.

Sears, John F. *Sacred Places: American Tourist Attractions in the Nineteenth Century.* New York: Oxford University Press, 1989.

Weidensaul, Scott. *Mountains of the Heart: A Natural History of the Appalachians.* Golden, Colo.: Fulcrum Publishing, 2000.

Weidensaul, Scott. *Seasonal Guide to the Natural Year.* Golden, Colo.: Fulcrum Publishing, 1993.

Wells, J. V. *Important Bird Areas in New York State.* Albany, N.Y.: National Audubon Society, 1998.

White, William Chapman. *Adirondack Country.* New York: Alfred A. Knopf, 1954.

Williams, Deborah. *Natural Wonders of New York: A Guide to Parks, Preserves, and Wild Places.* Castine, Maine: Country Roads Press, 1995.

INDEX

The boggy shoreline of Black Pond in the Calverton Ponds Preserve fosters a mix of maples, oaks, and pitch pines. Coastal plain ponds such as this are found on coastal outwash plains formed from runoff from the last glacial age. The only other similar habitat remaining in the world is in Siberia.

ABOUT THE AUTHOR

CHARLES BRUMLEY WAS born in Baltimore, Maryland, but all his life he spent a few summer weeks each year at his family's camp, which dates back to his great-grandparents, in the Adirondacks at Piseco Lake in Hamilton County. In 1984 Brumley moved from his farm in York County, Pennsylvania, to make a permanent home in the village of Saranac Lake in Adirondack Park. There he has worked as a social worker, an instructor of Adirondack history and social sciences at North Country Community College, and an outdoor guide. He is also the author of *Guides of the Adirondacks: A History,* as well as two collections of Adirondack short stories.

Brumley is an Adirondack 46er, having climbed all forty-six Adirondack peaks over four thousand feet, and he has participated in the ninety-mile Adirondack Canoe Classic twelve times. As of this writing, he has continued his streak of running a mile or more each day for twenty-seven years.

He notes that some years ago he and photographer Carl Heilman went head to head twice in a fourteen-mile snowshoe race; they finished in a tie each time. "My day is coming," Brumley says; he admits he has not raced on snowshoes in many years, however.

ABOUT THE PHOTOGRAPHER

CARL HEILMAN II has lived in the Adirondacks of upstate New York since 1973. He fell in love with the rugged character of the Adirondack mountains on his first climb in the High Peaks on a wild wintry day in 1975. Soon after, he bought his first camera to photograph the spectacular landscapes he was exploring. Since then, he has been photographing the wild natural landscape, working to capture on film the grandeur of the wilderness, as well as a sense of the emotional and spiritual connection he has with nature. His passion for spending time in some of the wildest regions of the Adirondacks became a lifelong quest to record on film the essence of a true wilderness experience and help convey that feeling to others. He now uses special panoramic equipment to capture his expansive 360-degree photographs of the natural landscape.

Carl's award-winning photographs have been published regionally and internationally in books, magazines, and calendars and a variety of commercial uses. His credits include *National Geographic Adventure, Backpacker, Outside, Nature Conservancy,* and *Adirondack Life.* He has presented many programs and exhibits throughout New York State, and his fine art prints are part of numerous collections. His book *Adirondacks: Views of An American Wilderness* was published by Rizzoli in 1999.